PRIMAR
PROFESSIONAL BO

DEVELOPING CHILDREN'S NON-FICTION WRITING

working with writing frames

MAUREEN LEWIS & DAVID WRAY

© 1995 David Wray and Maureen Lewis

234567890   678901234

Published by Scholastic Ltd
Villiers House
Clarendon Avenue
Leamington Spa
Warwickshire CV32 5PR

Authors David Wray and Maureen Lewis
Editor Ruth Nason
Series Designer Lynne Joesbury
Designer Toby Long

Designed using Aldus Pagemaker
Printed in Great Britain by Bell & Bain Ltd, Glasgow

The right of David Wray and Maureen Lewis to be identified as
the Authors of this Work has been asserted by them
in accordance with the Copyright, Designs
and Patents Act 1988

British Library Cataloguing-in-Publication Data
A catalogue record for this book is available from the British Library.

ISBN 0-590-53388-6

PRIMARY
PROFESSIONAL BOOKSHELF

CONTENTS

PRIMARY
PROFESSIONAL BOOKSHELF

ACKNOWLEDGEMENTS

The publishers gratefully acknowledge permission to reproduce the following copyright material:

Association for Science Education for *Discovering the Cure for Scurvy* by Joan Solomon (1989, Association for Science Education); Department of National Savings for 'Government Stock' from National Savings Investment Guide (1994, Department of National Savings); Crown copyright is reproduced with the permission of the Controller of HMSO for OFSTED (1993), DES report (1992), DES report (1975); Reed Books Australia for *Issues* by R. Martin (*Magic Bean* series, Heinemann, 1991); Thimble Press for *How Texts Teach What Readers Learn* by Margaret Meek (Thimble Press, 1988); 'How Lasers Work' reproduced from *New Technology, Lasers* by permission of Usborne Publishing Ltd © Usborne Publishing Ltd, 1984.

INTRODUCTION

DO YOU RECOGNISE THIS CHILD?

Zoe does not find writing easy, but she always tries hard to complete the task she has been set. On one occasion she was asked to research and write a report on whales and dolphins, as part of a class topic on 'Living Things'. She wrote diligently for half an hour, to produce this:

> Into The Blue
> Of the thirty-odd species of oceanic Dolphins none makes a more striking entrance than stenella attenuata the spotted dolphin. Under water spotted dolphins first app as white dots against the Blue. The beaks of the adults are whit - tipped and that distinctive blaze viewed head-on makes a perfect circle. When the vanguard of school is "echolocating" on you - examining you sonically - the beaks all swing your way, and each circular bbze reflects light before any of the rest of the animal dose. you see spots before your eyes.
>
> The word Bredanensis comes from the name of the artist van Brd who drew a portorate of the type spiee wich was stranded a Brest on the Brittany cost of france in 1823 the steno is in honour of the celebr seventeenth - century Danish anatomist Pr nilso lans steno.

After reading just a few lines of Zoe's work you probably recognised what had happened. She had copied, word for word, from an information book she had been consulting. When asked, she could not read 'her' writing back to the teacher and she had only the vaguest notion of what she had written.

Is this typical of primary children's non-fiction writing? We suspect that all teachers have experienced similar incidents in their classrooms. Zoe may be an extreme example, but we have all known occasions when certain pupils, faced with a non-fiction writing task, have found no other way of coping with the writing demands than to copy.

EXAMINING NON-FICTION WRITING

This book is about non-fiction writing in the classroom. It shows how teachers can use writing frames to give children a structure for their non-fiction writing. This approach helps children move towards greater independence in their writing, while also familiarising them with different forms of non-fiction texts.

In the following chapters we will look at the present state of writing in our classrooms and at the difficulties claimed to be inherent in writing non-fiction. We will look at the work of the Australian genre theorists and particularly at the ways in which their work enriches our knowledge about language. We will then discuss how this knowledge can be used to support our pupils' writing; and especially in view of the highlighting of the issue of range in the most recent National Curriculum orders for English, how it can help us to extend the variety of writing which we ask our children to produce. We will suggest a model of teaching that assists children in the transition from supported to independent writing.

In Chapter 5 we will present a range of writing frames, showing how to introduce them in the classroom. We will stress that writing frames are much more than simple worksheets, and will discuss how teachers might use them to the greatest effect. We will go on to look at how teachers might recognise when children are ready to stop using the frames, and what they might do then.

Our work with groups of teachers using writing frames has always been characterised by great excitement at the quality of non-fiction writing which many children have been able to produce. We hope that this sense of excitement comes across in the following pages, especially through the many examples of children's writing which we include.

We would like to thank the many teachers and children throughout the country who have trialled writing frames in their classrooms. Their insights, expertise, suggestions and critical support have been invaluable. We would particularly like to thank:

Carolyn Ballard, Bishopsteignton Primary School
Margaret Birch, Manor Primary School, Ivybridge
Andrea Bradshaw, Bere Alston County Primary School
Caroline Cox, Thornbury County Primary School
Rosie Culverhouse, Tavistock Community College
David Edwards, Stoke Hill Middle School
Jan Marshall, Horrabridge County Primary School
Patricia Rospigliosi, Learning Support Teacher, West Devon
Chris Stratton, Alphington Combined School

who were all members of our Genre Group and gave freely of their time, their ideas and their classroom experience.

We would also like to acknowledge the support of the Nuffield Foundation who funded the work of the Exeter Extending Literacy Project (EXEL).

CHAPTER 1

THE CURRENT STATE OF WRITING IN PRIMARY SCHOOLS

There has been a great deal of development in the nature of writing tasks which school children are asked to undertake and much exciting and innovative work is done, especially in the classrooms of teachers who took an active part in projects such as the National Writing Project and Language in the National Curriculum (LINC). However, from recent reports, it appears that the state of writing in British schools may not be as healthy as it might be. For example, in its summary report of inspections of the teaching of English, OFSTED (1993) claims that 'much remains to be done to improve the writing competence of pupils at all ages' (page 2) and goes on to say that 'writing standards ... were depressed by *excessive copying* and a lack of demand for *sustained, independent* and *extended* writing' (page 8, our italics). According to the previous year's report, Inspectors had also noted that 'room for further improvement remains; much of the required writing was of stories ... and there were few opportunities for *other kinds of writing'* (DES, 1992, page 14, our italics).

For the busy teacher trying to balance the many demands of the National Curriculum, such reports can make negative and depressing reading, especially when the concluding section, headed 'Issues', states bluntly:

> ... in the immediate future schools need to help teachers to acquire more knowledge and expertise in relation to:
> • knowledge about language – its structures, functions and variations;
> • teaching writing... (OFSTED, 1993, page 23)

The reports do not set out in any detail *how* schools are to reach these goals, but put forward general exhortations that they should address the issues and acknowledge the need for INSET and guidance. In this book we are particularly concerned with how teachers can achieve the laudable aims of increasing their own knowledge about language and improving their skills in teaching writing, so that their pupils become able to produce original, independent and sustained writing. Our focus is particularly on non-fiction writing. Why is this?

THE IMPORTANCE OF NON-FICTION TEXTS

Our literate society demands that we read and write a wide range of styles of texts. Many of the texts that adult members of society encounter and need to deal with every day are non-fiction texts. Today you may have read a newspaper, road signs, junk mail offering you double glazing, your bank statement, the latest National Curriculum circular, a note about playground duty, the instructions on the bottle of headache pills, and so on. You may have written a note explaining your absence from a meeting, filled in a form, drafted a report on a child about to be statemented, composed a letter to an old friend recounting the events of the last few days. You will have undertaken a wide variety of reading and writing, but the likelihood is that most of the texts you encountered or created were non-fiction texts. You may have read a novel for pleasure or written a short story, but the text types you saw and dealt with will have been *predominantly* non-fiction.

'But,' you might object, 'that's not true. I've read and written a lot of fiction today. I've shared lots of story books with readers. I've read a story to my class and we did some shared writing of a modern fairy-tale.' This is probably true for many teachers. A moment's reflection will confirm that such a major exposure to fiction texts is peculiar to the life of the classroom. Narrative texts play an important role in our classrooms and it is no part of our aim in this book to suggest that story and narrative are not essential parts of children's literacy experiences. Work such as that of Gordon Wells (1987) has taught us beyond doubt, how crucial the experience of story is in the literacy development of young children. We would suggest, however, that we need to give rather more thought to the role of non-fiction texts, if we are to prepare our pupils for encounters with writing outside the confines of the classroom.

Much of the last few decades' research into the development of children's writing has tended to concentrate on personal and fictional texts (as our brief historical review later in this chapter will show), while non-fiction writing has been relatively neglected. The demand that children 'read and respond to all kinds of writing' (DES, 1990, page 7) and the emphasis on 'range' in the latest National Curriculum orders for English mean that we need to look closely at how we can help our pupils become aware of different non-fiction text types, and develop into competent writers of such text themselves. Our work with teachers as part of the Exeter Extending Literacy (EXEL) project has made it clear to us that increasing children's interactions with non-fiction texts is an area of current concern, and that there is a particular wish to widen the range and quality of children's non-fiction writing.

TEACHERS' VIEWS ON NON-FICTION WRITING

A survey of teachers' views and attitudes on literacy matters (Lewis and Wray, 1995) undertaken at the start of the EXEL project, revealed interesting data about the current thinking and practices of teachers in the areas of reading and writing. In one section of the survey 130 teachers were asked about their aims in developing children's writing, any significant problems that concerned them in this area, and the teaching activities and materials they currently used.

Over 95 per cent of the teachers questioned agreed strongly with the comment that 'Children need to write for a range of audiences and in a range of styles in order to become effective writers'. In the subsequent interviews, when they were asked to talk about their aims and problems in teaching writing, most teachers tended to concentrate their replies on the writing of narrative texts. The writing of specifically non-fiction texts was mentioned by only 15 per cent of the sample. About 55 per cent did talk about the need to introduce children to a range of texts, but having articulated this awareness, they went on to list only a limited range of text types and again these were often 'fiction' – poetry and different types of stories, for example. The few teachers who mentioned non-fiction text types did so mostly in relation to curriculum areas. For instance, writing in science or in history. Only one teacher mentioned any non-fiction text type by name: they identified 'reports' and 'explanations'. All this suggests a general lack of knowledge of the range of texts and, at the least, a lack of a shared vocabulary with which to discuss text types. It supports the hypothesis of OFSTED, that teachers need to improve their own knowledge about the 'structures, functions and variations' of language.

One problem in relation to writing which teachers in the survey mentioned (excluding the problems of time and resources reported by almost 100 per cent of them!), was that of helping children to move away from copying. As one teacher put it, 'I always try to encourage them to write in their own words, but you still find children taking it straight from the page of a book.' This echoes OFSTED's concern about 'excessive copying'.

Our work with teachers during the EXEL project has confirmed this measure of agreement between what teachers themselves and school inspectors see as the problems to be tackled in teaching children to read and write non-fiction texts. Having identified problem areas, we have been working with teachers in their classrooms throughout the country to develop ways of helping children to write original, independent and extended pieces of non-fiction.

APPROACHES TO THE TEACHING
OF WRITING

The teaching of writing has, of course, been an area of interest and debate for a long while, but in recent years the National Curriculum has made more explicit what is expected within the primary classroom. There is still discussion and controversy over some of its emphases but, in general, the National Curriculum English document has appeared to build upon principles and practices that have evolved over the last 25 to 30 years. The general rubric to the writing Attainment Target, for example, states that we should aim to produce writers with 'a growing ability to construct and convey meaning in written language, matching style to audience and purpose' (DES, 1990, page 12).

The emphasis on form (the characteristics of different text types), audience and purpose was elaborated throughout the statements of attainment. We read in the statements of attainment for non-fiction writing, Levels 1–5, the requirement for children to 'move from the ability to produce simple, coherent, non-chronological writing' (SAT 2d) to the stage of being able to 'write in a variety of forms for a range of purposes and audiences' (SAT 5a). In the 1995 version of the orders (DFE, 1995), such detailed attainment targets are no longer given but the general requirements for all key stages still make clear that 'to develop as effective writers, pupils should be taught to use ... a widening variety of forms for different purposes' (page 2). These orders are explicit in their requirement for teachers to provide children with non-fiction writing experiences that introduce them to the 'characteristics of different types of writing' (page 15).

Expecting children to understand form, audience and purpose is a relatively new development in the teaching of writing. In Chapters 2 and 3 we will look in some detail at how the recent work of the genre theorists can help us increase our knowledge of the generic forms of non-fiction and of how writing for specific purposes and/or audiences influences the form which the text takes. First it will be useful to sketch the story of the teaching of writing, focusing on the changes that have led to the view that purpose, audience and form should be considered when a writing task is undertaken.

CHANGES IN THE TEACHING OF WRITING

Since the implementation of the 1944 Education Act there have been dramatic changes in approaches to the teaching of writing. The writing diet of some 1950's primary classrooms, consisting of formal, grammar-based exercises, writing stories with titles such as 'A day in the life of a penny' and non-fiction writing such as the copying out of information texts, came increasingly under attack throughout that decade: it was criticised as arid and unlikely to produce confident and independent writers. These criticisms gradually gave rise to what can loosely be called the 'creative writing' movement of the 1960s and early 1970s.

THE CREATIVE WRITING MOVEMENT

A range of expressions such as 'free writing', 'intensive writing' and 'imaginative writing' were used by various authors and commentators to describe the processes involved in creative writing in the classroom. The approach was characterised by encouraging a personal response to a stimulus – provided by the teacher or based on the children's own experiences. As class teachers during the latter part of this movement, we recall spending hours browning treasure maps in the oven to provide a convincing document to share with our class, passing round a richly embroidered shawl, playing music, even letting off fireworks in the classroom – all to provide the stimulus which would unlock a piece of creative writing from the souls of our pupils! At its best, this movement brought to the fore the idea that writing could be a personal response and it made clear that the motivation to write had a significant effect on the standard of children's writing. Books such as Clegg's *The Excitement of Writing* (1965) provided clear evidence of the quality of writing that such an approach could produce. Several other important books (Maybury, 1967; Lane and Kemp, 1967) added impetus to the movement and there appeared to be 'a general growth in awareness in the ways teachers ... approached their work on children's writing' (Beard, 1984).

However, the creative writing movement inevitably concentrated on poetic and fictional writing as opposed to factual work. This approach to teaching writing was criticised for leading, at worst, to work that 'is often false, artificially stimulated and pumped up by the teacher or written to an unconscious model which he has given to the children' (DES, 1975, page 163). The report in which that criticism appeared (usually called the 'Bullock Report') claimed that 'There is now more healthy scepticism about the value of this emphasis when it is at the expense of *other kinds of writing*.' (our italics). It showed an increased awareness of the need to work on improving the quality of a wider range of writing and also re-emphasised the importance of intention (purpose).

> We have already placed special emphasis on the importance of the pupil's intention as a writer and have suggested that this will arise out of the context of work in the class or the broader one of his out-of school life (DES, 1975, page 165).

BEGINNING TO WIDEN THE RANGE

Another important influence on the teaching of writing began to emerge during the 1970s. The narrowness of the creative writing approach was highlighted by James Britton (1972) who suggested that language could usefully be categorised into three rhetorical modes − expressive, transactional and poetic. The expressive mode is characterised as language 'close to the speaker' and is used to verbalise the writer's consciousness. The 'transactional mode is the language of 'getting things done': for example, giving instructions, attempting to persuade and advise, and passing on information. The poetic mode is language patterned in a particular way, as an artistic medium. That is the mode focused on in creative writing. Britton argued that children write first and most easily in the expressive mode, and that they gradually gain control over the other modes. He also pointed out that a child's writing may occur at transitional points between modes. Britton's work has been influential in two ways: it has given a theoretical framework to the idea that writing is for a wider range of purposes than just creative expression, and it has foregrounded the importance of the expressive mode in children's writing.

Britton *et al.* (1975) also suggested that children should write for a wider range of audiences than 'the teacher as examiner', who he discovered was the dominant audience in primary classrooms at that time. The Bullock Report made the same point:

> One further feature which is no less important ... is the nature of the 'audience' to which the writing is addressed ... we welcome the development to encourage writing for audiences outside the classroom (DES, 1975, page 166).

DEVELOPMENTAL AND PROCESS WRITING

During the 1980's two fresh perspectives on the teaching of writing became influential. The work of Donald Graves and his colleagues at the University of New Hampshire (Graves, 1983; Calkins, 1983) drew our attention to issues of purpose, context and audience in writing and, in particular, highlighted the *process* of writing as opposed to a previous emphasis on writing products. This was seen to include several kinds of thinking and activity, including planning, drafting, revision, editing and publication. Where teachers were influenced by this perspective, children became involved in a great deal of drafting and in its associated teaching procedure of conferencing.

Researchers working from the new theoretical perspective of emergent literacy put forward the view that people use language and literacy in their everyday lives and that this applies just as much to young children as it does to adults. Many studies began to appear which explored what very young children knew about literacy processes (Teale and Sulzby, 1986;

Hall, 1987), and the consensus was that their knowledge was considerable. Particularly from the work of Harste, Woodward and Burke (1984), the idea became widely accepted that children's early writing, often dismissed previously as 'scribble', was serving exactly the same purpose for them as adult writing does for adults: it was a means of creating meaning and thus of making sense of the surrounding world. Studies also suggested that, if children in school were given experience of using writing for meaningful purposes, then they would fairly naturally develop their understanding of and expertise in the technical demands of writing (Newman, 1984). Most famously, this view gave rise to a developmental approach to spelling, but it led also to assumption that children would naturally learn from experience how to write different types of text.

The National Writing Project took up and disseminated many of these ideas. Purpose and audience were strongly emphasised and suggestions were made regarding the need for explicit work on text structures. However, there was still an overwhelming concentration on the story form and little work was done on non-fiction texts. Discussions did begin to stress the issue of range in writing, but usually this consisted simply of listing a range of text types (Wray and Medwell, 1991).

The first version of the National Curriculum English document made it clear that children should undertake a wide range of different types of writing and that they should be 'helped to plan and produce these types of writing ... descriptions, explanations, opinions etc' (DES, 1990, page 37). Nonetheless, such pronouncements beg the question of whether children (and indeed their teachers) understand the *differences* between an explanation and an argument, a report and a discussion, and are familiar with the generic structures of these types of writing. Work currently being undertaken by a group of largely Australian academics, loosely called the 'genre theorists', has provided a way of looking at features of text beyond the level of the sentence and this important knowledge about language is discussed more fully in the next two chapters.

CHAPTER 2

GENRE THEORY: NEW INSIGHTS, NEW APPROACHES

In Chapter 1 we outlined some major developments from the last few decades in the understanding about and teaching of children's writing. There has been an increasing interest in the idea of encouraging children to write in an appropriate form, for a known audience and a particular purpose. However, what constitutes an appropriate form is often dealt with in very general terms. In the original version of the National Curriculum for English, for instance, the attainment targets for writing include the requirement for children to 'write in a variety of forms for a range of purposes and audiences' (DES, 1990, page 13). It is suggested, for example, that they 'write notes, letters, instructions, stories and poems in order to plan, inform, explain, entertain and express attitudes or emotions'.

Listing text types in this way implies that teachers and children know what distinguishes one form from another. At a certain level, of course, this is true. We all know what a story is like and how it differs from a recipe. Most of us are aware that a narrative usually has a beginning, a series of events and an ending, and many teachers discuss such ideas with their pupils, spending time working on openings or endings of narratives, for instance. However, it is still relatively rare for teachers of primary pupils to discuss non-fiction texts in such a way – that is, drawing on their knowledge of the usual structure of a particular text type in order to improve the children's writing of that form.

Recently a group of linguists including Gunther Kress, Jim Martin, Joan Rothery and Frances Christie have argued that we have quite an extensive unconscious knowledge of text types and their characteristics. It has been one aspect of their work to make this knowledge more explicit. These theorists are often loosely referred to as 'genre theorists' and their work is known as 'genre theory'.

A FUNCTIONAL APPROACH TO LANGUAGE

The genre theorists base their work on a functional approach to language. Such an approach looks at the ways in which language enables us to do things. It argues that we develop language in order to satisfy our needs in society. Based on Michael Halliday's work on children's language (1975, 1978, 1985), a functional language approach suggests that, as we use language, three things happen:

◆ we learn language;
◆ we learn through language;
◆ we learn about language.

If we think about our own language development from our earliest years, we can see that we *learn language* largely through using it. For example, we refine and add to our vocabulary by constant interaction with other language users. As we get older, we add to our knowledge of our language by reading and writing as well as by talking.

We use language to interact with our world and increase our knowledge of it. We develop concepts, ask questions, and make things happen through the medium of language. In other words, we *learn through language*.

As we use language, we acquire an implicit knowledge about how language itself works. For example, young children usually learn about plurals and begin to add an 's' to the ends of words, in their speech, long before they are formally 'taught' plurals as an item of grammar. Similarly, most children learn to distinguish between past and present tenses and use tenses appropriately before they receive any formal instruction in this area. As we use language, we *learn about language*. We now recognise that children come to school with an unconscious knowledge of language structures and their usage.

A functional language approach argues that our implicit knowledge about language should be brought out into the open, so that we can use it in our classrooms. One aspect of our implicit knowledge is our knowledge about genre.

WHAT IS 'GENRE'?

Over the last few years, as the work of certain teachers and academics has become more widely known, more of us have grown aware of the term 'genre'. Not long ago, had we been asked to define 'genre', we probably would have replied only in terms of books or films. We are all familiar with the idea of categorising books or films with certain common characteristics as 'romance' or 'murder mysteries' or 'westerns' or ' horror'. The genre theorists would argue that such book and film genres are just a few of the many different types that operate in our societies, and that the term 'genre' can be applied to a much wider range of language-based activities.

They see all texts, written and spoken, as being 'produced in response to, and out of, particular social situations and their specific structures' (Kress and Knapp, 1992, page 5). As a result, they put stress on the social and cultural factors that form a text, as well as on its linguistic features. They see a text as always a social object, and the making of a text as a 'social process' (ibid.). They argue that, in any society, there are certain social encounters, situations and events which recur constantly. As these 'events' are repeated over and over again, certain types of text – written and spoken – are created over and over again. These texts become recognised by the members of the society and, once recognised, they become conventionalised. We can see how this operates by looking at forms of greeting. If we meet an acquaintance in the street, a common exchange might be:

'Oh. hello. How are you?'

'I'm fine, thanks. How are you?'

'Fine... I'm fine. We must get together for a drink some time.'

'Good idea. I'll ring you.'

'Great. Look forward to it. Nice to see you. Bye.'

We all recognise this conventional exchange and instinctively 'know' the responses that are expected of us. We 'know' that we usually respond briefly and counter-question when asked how we are. Yet nobody has ever explicitly taught us this text. We have learned it through usage on similar occasions when it has been necessary to create a text for the purpose of acknowledging someone's presence without getting involved in a conversation. If our purpose were different (if, for example, we wanted to get involved in a more intimate conversation), we would structure our text in a different way. Our lives are full of such examples, when similar purposes and situations produce similar texts.

The genre theorists argue that texts have 'a high degree of internal structure' (Kress, 1982, page 98). This remains largely invisible to the reader/speaker because, when texts have become conventionalised (with recognisable rules and forms), they appear to have an existence of their own – they appear 'natural'. Genre theory identifies the larger structures of a whole text, what Kress calls the 'linguistic features beyond the sentence' (ibid. page 97), and also studies the language features within these larger structures.

Many genre theorists take their argument further. Their point is not only that we can recognise generic structures of texts, but that we should make our unconscious knowledge of these structures explicit; that these forms and their social meanings 'can and should be taught' (Kress and Knapp, 1992, page 4). The idea that this knowledge of structures should be explicitly taught is controversial (Barrs, 1991/92; Stratta and Dixon, 1992; Cairney, 1992), for it begs the question of why and how. We will return to these issues in Chapters 3 and 4. We will also look more closely at the theorists' analysis of the 'internal structures' of certain non-fiction genres.

PURPOSE AND GENRE

Many commentators have defined 'genre'. Some say it is the schematic structure found in a text: 'By genre, we mean the overall structuring of the text which characterises different forms of communication' (Harrison and McEvedy, 1987, page 55). More commonly it is argued that the form a text takes is influenced by its purpose. Look at these definitions of genre:

✦ a social process which has some purpose (Collerson, 1988, page 12);

✦ a purposeful communicative activity (Littlefair, 1992, page 10);

✦ any staged and culturally purposive activity leading to the creation of a text ... to serve different social purposes (Martin, Christie and Rothery, 1987, page 59).

Notice how the purpose of the communication is central to these definitions. Genre theory claims that texts (written or spoken) are structured according to their purpose and texts with the same purpose will have the same schematic structure.

In practice, what does this idea of generic structures being determined by purpose actually mean? Let's take a text type with which we are all familiar – instructions, or 'procedural texts', as we will call them from now on. The purpose of procedural texts is to tell someone how to do something, as in recipes, instruction leaflets about machines, DIY leaflets, and so on. This purpose gives rise to the particular form of procedural texts: they have to make clear what it is you are doing or making, what materials you need to achieve this aim and the steps you should take to reach a successful conclusion. The purpose would not be served by a different arrangement of the text; if, for example, the instructions were given first, followed by the list of materials you needed, and finally the information as to what it was you were making. The schematic structure of a procedural text helps achieve its purpose and is therefore usually:

✦ goal;

✦ materials;

✦ steps to achieve the goal (usually in chronological order).

You will be aware of such a structure in recipes and DIY guides. You may not have been explicitly aware of it in other procedural ('how to') texts, but, if you examine them, you will see that, on the whole, they also follow the pattern outlined above. You will also be using a similar generic structure when you give any spoken instructions. Imagine yourself giving instructions to your class at the beginning of a session:

> Today we're going to finish writing our stories *(goal)*,
>
> so you'll need your jotters, pencils, line guides and best paper *(materials)*. When you've got those sorted out, get on and see if you can finish your first draft. Then you can share it with your writing partner or with me and discuss any alterations you think need to be made. Don't forget to check spellings at the end. OK, off you go *(instructions)*.

It is highly unlikely that you consciously planned to use, or were even aware of using, the schematic structure of a procedural text. Your purpose (to tell the children what to do) meant that you 'automatically' used it; it came 'naturally'. When we look at how the schematic structure of a text helps it to achieve its purpose, we are considering its genre.

GENRE AND CULTURE

We have seen earlier that the creation of a text takes place within a culture or society. It is in the context of a certain society that we have a purpose for creating a text, and that purpose gives rise to a text produced in a particular genre. If genres are formed within societies, then they can vary from society to society, even if the purpose is the same. The genre for shopping is a good example of this type of variation. Within any society the purpose of the language exchange accompanying shopping is to buy and sell. In Western European society the generic structure of a shopping text would generally follow this form:

> 'Good morning.' *(mutual greeting)*
>
> 'Can I help you?' *(query)*

'I'd like...' *(shopping request)*

'Certainly. What colour would you like?...' *(granting of request)*

'That will be...' *(statement of price)*

'Thank you. Goodbye.' *(completing transaction)*

However, in different societies there are different norms. There may, for instance, be an expectation of some bartering over the price; or extended pleasantries may be essential before any mention is made of a transaction. In these circumstances a different text will be found, with a different generic structure from the Western European model. The purpose is the same and the genre is the same, but the generic structure is different. It is perhaps when we enter different societies that we realise most clearly how 'learned' our own generic structures, which we normally take for granted, really are. We have all had experiences of situations where we have not 'known the script', say when ordering a meal in a foreign country and we have been aware of making the wrong responses, getting the pace wrong, and so on. We understand then that text structures are not automatic or natural but something that has to be learned.

GENRE AND REGISTER

Every text has both a genre and a register. Figure 2.1 shows Derewianka's idea of the relationship between culture, genre and register.

Genre refers to the overall structure and form of a text. 'Register' results from particular choices about language which are made as the text is created. These choices will depend upon several contextual features, each of which has been given a term in functional grammar. These features are:

✦ the *tenor*, that is, the relationship between the participants – text producers and receivers;

✦ the *mode*, that is, the channel of communication being used – for example, speech or writing;

✦ the *field*, that is, the subject-matter of the text.

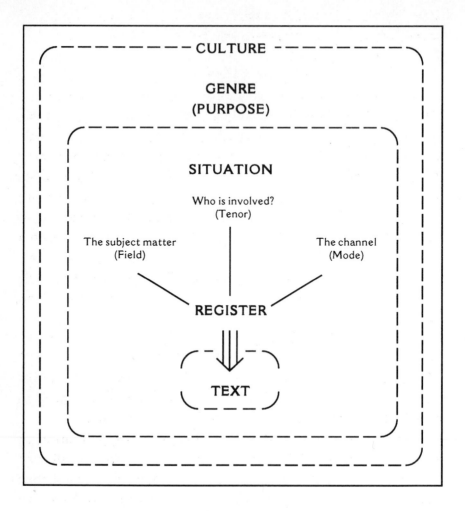

Figure 2.1. Derewianka's diagram showing the relationship between culture, genre and register in any text.

TENOR

The tenor of a text depends on the relationship between the participants in the text creation: the producer of the text and its recipient(s) or audience. The tenor can range from formal to informal, friendly to unfriendly, and is influenced by such factors as the relative status and ages of the participants, how well they know each other, how they feel towards each other. These factors will be reflected in the style of language used, from intimate forms of address, including colloquial terms, to something much more correct and polite.

MODE

The mode, or channel of communication, may be either writing or speech; but there are many variations within those, depending on factors such as the distance in time and space between the participants, whether the communication is face-to-face or consists of something recorded to be read or listened to at a later date, and whether the communication accompanies an action as it happens or is distanced from it. Are you and your partner discussing where to hang a picture as you stand with a hammer and nail in your hand? Are you discussing this as you stand in front of the print shop window? Or are you describing the discussion to a friend after it has taken place and the picture has been hung?

FIELD

The field refers to the subject-matter of the text – the what, who, when, how, why, where. The subject-matter will give rise to specific vocabulary.

Tenor, mode and field interact to give a text its particular register. Halliday (1978, page 32) describes register as referring to 'the fact that the language we speak or write varies according to the type of situation'. An example will help to make all this more concrete.

Let us imagine that you wish to argue the case for replacing the reading scheme currently used in your school. Your purpose is to persuade someone else to accept your point of view. You will use a persuasive genre and the generic structure will look something like this:

✦ an opening statement *(your thesis)*;

✦ reasons and/or evidence to back up your point of view *(points and elaboration)*;

✦ a summary and a re-statement of your opening position *(reiteration)*;

GENRE (PERSUASIVE)

REGISTER

When talking to parents	When talking to headteacher
↓	↓

Tenor

Expert to non-expert
Slightly known to each other
High status (teacher)/lower status (parent)
Language would have personal pronouns but no intimate forms of address. Probably a little formal.

Tenor

Expert to expert
Well-known to each other
High status (headteacher) lower status (teacher)
Language would have personal pronouns, maybe first names. Friendly but business-like.

Mode

Spoken
Face to face
Distanced action
i.e. arguing for something to happen in the future.

Mode

Spoken
Face to face
Distanced action
i.e. arguing for something to happen in the future.

Field

Reading schemes
Would include field-specific but not over-technical vocabulary, for example, letter sounds, guessing the meaning from the rest of the sentence, guessing the meaning from the way the language is used.

Field

Reading schemes
Would include field-specific technical vocabulary, for example, phonics, context clues, syntax cues.

Figure 2.2. Diagram to show how register can differ within the same generic structure.

This overall generic form would stay the same whether you were talking to your headteacher or to a parents' meeting, but the register of the text would vary considerably. Figure 2.2 summarises and explains this variation.

WRITTEN GENRES IN THE CLASSROOM

Different theorists have categorised in different ways the written genres that are commonly used in the classroom. Collerson (1988), for example, suggests a separation into *Early genres* (labels, observational comment, recount and narratives) and *Factual genres* (procedures, reports, explanations, and arguments or exposition). Wing Jan (1991) divides texts into *Factual* (reports, explanations, procedures, persuasive writing, interviews, surveys, descriptions, biographies, recounts and narrative information) and *Fictional* (traditional fiction and contemporary modern fiction).

There is, however, a large measure of agreement as to what are the main non-fiction genres. During our classroom work with teachers, and for the purposes of this book, we have taken as our model the categories of non-fiction genres identified by the Sydney linguists (Martin and Rothery, 1980, 1981, 1986) and subsequently developed in Australian schools (Callaghan and Rothery, 1988; Macken *et al.*, 1989). Part of the work of this group was to collect and analyse non-fiction texts, including many examples of children's school scripts. From this they identified six important non-fiction genres which we use in our culture, and discovered that, in schools, one of these genres was overwhelmingly predominant.

The six main types of non-fiction genre they identified were:
+ recount;
+ report;
+ procedure;
+ explanation;
+ persuasion or exposition;
+ discussion.

In Chapter 3 we will look more closely at each of these

genres and will reveal which one was discovered to be the dominant written genre in classrooms. Can you predict which it will be?

We must stress that the idea of there being six main types of non-fiction genre does not mean that there are only six non-fiction genres in our society. There are many different genres and more will be created as new writing needs and media arise. There are also many examples of mixed genres.

THE CREATION OF NEW GENRES

If genres are created within societies, it follows that as societies change, so genres will change. Furthermore, if genres arise from particular purposes, then new genres will arise to fulfil the requirements of new purposes. We can see this happening in the texts created using computers. As people communicate more frequently by electronic mail, so they are creating new vocabulary and generic structures to make the purpose of a text explicit. If your purpose when using electronic mail is to express a particular emotion, say anger, the generic structure of such a text will be:

> (Opening emotion indicator) <Flame on>
>
> <Message>
>
> (Closing emotion indicator) <Flame off>

Computer users 'know', through practice, that this form indicates a particularly strongly felt emotion. Otherwise the message would be typed unadorned. Ten years ago this particular generic form did not exist.

Initially, the genre theorists claimed that 'there is a small and fixed number of genres in any written tradition' (Kress, 1982, page 98). They now concede that there are not a fixed number of genres and that genres are rather dynamic and fluid structures.

CHAPTER 3

THE GENRES OF NON-FICTION

Discussing narrative forms is established practice in our classrooms. We introduce children to the idea that stories have a beginning, a middle and an end, and we spend time working with them on, for example, alternative openings such as 'Once upon a time', 'It was a dark and stormy night' and 'Every day of the week '. Perhaps we analyse with our pupils the traditional forms of fairy tales – looking at how they are based on themes such as a task being set or the ways in which different people react to a 'chance' meeting with a stranger in need. We may talk about the vocabulary used in such tales and how the events take place within time. We are used to helping children to write in narrative and poetic forms. We do so by conducting explicit discussion about the language features of stories and poems, in book talk and conferencing, and by trying to immerse the children in examples of these forms of writing. We read them plenty of stories and poems, we keep a good supply of attractive story and poetry books in the classroom, and we make strenuous efforts to 'sell' the books to children, including by encouraging them to take books home.

Gunther Kress (1982) argued that children learning to write need to know about the broad structures as well as the smaller units of text, and he also pointed out the relationship between genres and smaller text elements. We regularly ask pupils to attempt writing in narrative and, to a smaller degree, poetic forms, and often, to develop their understanding of and expertise in writing, we start by discussing the features of these forms, that is, their generic structural characteristics. It is far less likely, however, that we will discuss non-fiction texts in such a way. One of the main reasons for this, and one of the major motivations for writing this book, is that until recently there has been little explicit knowledge among primary teachers of how non-fiction texts are organised. As competent language users we all instinctively 'know' how to write an explanation of why an event has happened, and how that form of writing differs from, for example, writing a set of instructions; but we have had no shared vocabulary for talking about these different written forms. The work of researchers including Christie, Rothery and Martin has provided such a vocabulary. Their analysis of the characteristics of the main non-fiction genres has opened the way for us to discuss the features of non-fiction writing.

THE GENERIC STRUCTURES OF NON-FICTION TEXTS

The main non-fiction text types are described as recount, report, explanation, procedure, persuasion and discussion. The remainder of this chapter looks at the purpose of each of these genres, its structure and language features. Examples are given from children's writing and from published texts.

RECOUNT GENRE

THE PURPOSE OF RECOUNTS

Recounts are written to retell events, with the purpose of either informing or entertaining – or even with both purposes!

THE GENERIC STRUCTURE OF RECOUNTS

A recount usually consists of:

◆ a 'scene-setting' opening (orientation)

> I went on a visit to the museum ...
>
> Our class planted some seeds ...

◆ a recount of the events as they occurred (events)

> I sat with Sarah on the bus...
>
> We put soil in four pots...

◆ a closing statement (reorientation)

> When we got back from the trip we wrote about it.
>
> The seeds with soil, light and water grew best.

THE LANGUAGE FEATURES OF RECOUNTS

Recounts are usually written:

✦ in the past tense

> The Romans landed in Britain in....

✦ in chronological order

> They established a camp and then began to...

✦ with a particular person or people as the subject of the action

> After that the general ordered the legion to march...

✦ using doing/action clauses

> landed, established, ordered... to march.

The recounts genre is used for biographies, autobiographies and history texts. An example of a child's recount writing is given in Figure 3.1 and an example of published recount writing in Figure 3.2.

REPORT GENRE

THE PURPOSE OF REPORTS

Reports are written to describe the way things are. They can be about a range of natural, cultural or social subject.

THE GENERIC STRUCTURE OF REPORTS

A report usually consists of:

✦ an opening, general classification

> Exeter is a city in Devon.
>
> Humans are mammals.

✦ a more technical classification (optional)

> A city holds a Royal Charter.
>
> The scientific name is Homo Sapiens.

✦ a description of the subject, which might refer to qualities, habits/behaviour, parts and their function.

> Exeter is situated on the river Exe. The city is the county town of Devon. It has the university, law courts, County Hall, the headquarters of several large companies and local TV and radio stations within its boundaries. County Hall is the administrative centre for Devon County Council and it is from there that...

Our trip to Exeter Museum	
On Tuesday the 1st February we went on a school trip to a Roman museum in Exeter.	ORIENTATION
First of all we split in to 2 groups. Then my group went upstairs. We looked at Roman tiles, bits of pottery, jawbones, a deer antler, a coin, sheep bone, and a bit of mosaic. We saw a tile which, before it was baked, a dog walked over and it had paw prints on it. When we went downstairs into the Roman kitchen which had been reconstructed from information from the ground. We did some observational drawings. Then we each had a turn at grinding the flour. The guide who took us around told us to look for a mysterious animal that the Romans ate. I was the first person to find out what it was. It was a hedgehog. Then we went to another museum. It was much better than the first because the man who took us round was funny and we allowed to try on Roman armour. We handled the weapons as well. There was a sword, a dagger and a pilon. The armour was a breast plate, a shield, a helmet and a belt made with leather and chingles. The bits they hadn't got were the helmet, dagger and shield. Then we looked at a part of a mosaic. Then we went home.	EVENTS
It was a good trip. I liked the armour.	REORIENTATION
Amy – Year 4	

Figure 3.1. Child's recount writing.

Magellan set out on his voyage around the world in 1519.	ORIENTATION
He started from Seville in Spain with five ships: fifteen weeks later they managed to get round the tip of South America, through the Straits of Magellan, and into the Pacific. By now his men were in a terrible state. They were so short of food that they were eating sawdust and chewing leather. They also had the new disease which made their mouths sore and swollen. Finally in the Philippine Islands those who survived feasted on strange new fruits such as bananas and coconuts which they had never tasted before, and all of them recovered. There were far more deaths on this trip from fighting and treachery. Magellan himself was killed, and only one ship returned to Spain more than three years after they had set out. That one ship was so laden with cloves that the sale of its cargo was enough to make a rich profit for the ship's owners.	EVENTS
There are many such stories of illness and death on all the long voyages of discovery.	REORIENTATION

Figure 3.2. Example of recount.
From: Discovering the Cure for Scurvy *by Joan Solomon. The Association for Science Education, 1989*

THE LANGUAGE FEATURES OF REPORTS

Reports are usually written

◆ in the present tense

◆ focusing on groups of things, 'generic participants'

> a city, mammals

◆ using 'being' and 'having' clauses

> Exeter is, it has

The report genre is common in science and geography text books and in encyclopaedias. An example of a child's report writing is given in Figure 3.3 and an example of published report writing in Figure 3.4.

Lungs	
Our lungs are organs in our body which do the breathing.	**GENERAL CLASSIFICATION**
The lungs are divided into sections called Lobes. There are 2 lobes in the left lung, and 3 lobes in the right lung. Inside each lobe, the lung tubes split and split again, and soon look like this:- (here Simon had drawn a diagram) At the end of the lung is a 'bubble' called an alveolur. When we breathe in, the oxygen enters our blood via the alveolur, and when we breathe out, the carbon dioxide leaves us in the same way. When we smoke, the Alveoli get clogged up with tar, so we cannot breathe properly.	**DESCRIPTION**
Simon – Year 6	

Figure 3.3. Child's report writing.

Government Stock Gilts are marketable securities issued by the Government.	**GENERAL CLASSIFICATION**
They offer regular income at fixed nominal rates (some are also index-linked), and the opportunity of a tax-free capital gain. But, their value can go down as well as up — see our booklet on Government Stock. New issues of Gilts are purchased direct from the Bank of England but can be registered on the National Savings Stock Register (NSSR). Existing Gilts can be bought or sold through the NSSR, a stockbroker, or a bank. All our transactions are handled by post. Interest on Gilts is taxable but Gilts held on the NSSR pay gross interest automatically. Capital gains arising from the sale or redemption of Gilts are exempt from Capital Gains Tax. Our latest booklet has full details and an application form. To send off for a copy, turn to the Priority Request Form on page 29, or call us during office hours on 0645-645000. Calls are charged at your local rate.	**DESCRIPTION**

Figure 3.4. Example of report text from: National Savings Investment Guide, Department of National Savings, 1994. Available at all Post Offices.

EXPLANATION GENRE

THE PURPOSE OF EXPLANATIONS

Explanations describe natural or social processes or how something works.

THE GENERIC STRUCTURE OF EXPLANATIONS

Explanations usually consist of:

✦ a general statement to introduce the topic

> A butterfly goes through several stages in its life cycle.
>
> Computers use a binary number system.

✦ a series of logical steps explaining how or why something occurs

> The adult butterfly lays eggs on a suitable leaf. The eggs hatch and a caterpillar emerges. The caterpillar begins to feed and when it is fully grown it...

The Water Cycle	
The water cycle is about what happens to water. I want to explain where rain comes from.	OPENING STATEMENT
To begin with the sun shines on the sea and turns it into water vapour and the water vapour rises up into the sky. Next the wind blows it and it turns into clouds. Then as it gets colder the water vapour condenses back into water. This falls as rain. It runs down the hills and under the earth and into the rivers and seas. Finally it starts again.	SERIES OF STEPS EXPLAINING THE SUBJECT
Bill – Year 5.	

Figure 3.5. Child's explanation writing.

How laser discs work	OPENING STATEMENT

The picture shows a laser disc being scanned by a semiconductor laser chip. Some players use small HeNe lasers instead. It also shows the optical equipment of lenses, mirrors and so on which are inside the player.
    The laser disc has a very reflective metallic surface, covered by a protective coating of clear plastic. There are microscopically tiny indentations in this surface, called 'pits' and the plain areas in between are 'flats'. The circle on the right shows the pits and flats greatly magnified.
    The player spins the disc and scans it with the laser beam, which moves straight across the disc from the centre to the edge. The shiny surface reflects the beam back into the player, where it is picked up by an electronic device. This produces an electrical signal when it detects light.
    The pits and flats on the disc reflect the laser beam differently, producing a varying beam. This in turn makes the detector produce a varying electrical signal, which the player de-codes back into video pictures and sounds.
	SERIES OF STEPS EXPLAINING THE SUBJECT

Figure 3.6. Example of an explanation from: How Lasers Work, in New Technology, Lasers *(Usborne Publishing, 1984).*

THE LANGUAGE FEATURES OF EXPLANATIONS

Explanations are often written:

✦ in the simple present tense

    lays, hatch

✦ using temporal connectives

    then, next, after, etc.

✦ and/or using causal connectives

    because, therefore etc.

✦ using mainly action clauses

    the eggs hatch, a caterpillar emerges.

The explanation genre is often found in science, geography, history and social science text-books. An example of a child's explanation writing is given in Figure 3.5 and an example of a published explanation in Figure 3.6.

PROCEDURAL GENRE

THE PURPOSE OF PROCEDURES

Procedures or instructions describe how something is done through a series of sequenced steps.

THE GENERIC STRUCTURE OF PROCEDURES

A procedural text is often accompanied by a diagram or illustration and usually consists of:

✦ a statement of what is to be achieved

    How to make a sponge cake

✦ a list of materials/equipment needed to achieve the goal

    2 eggs

    4 ounces of self-raising flour

✦ a series of sequenced steps to achieve the goal

    Cream the sugar and butter...

THE LANGUAGE FEATURES OF PROCEDURES

Procedures are usually written:

✦ in the simple present tense or the imperative

    First you sift the flour

    Sift the flour

✦ in chronological order

    first, next, after that

✦ focusing on generalised human agents rather than individuals

    First you take, *rather than* First I take

✦ using mainly doing/action clauses.

    cream the butter, sift the flour.

The procedural genre is commonly found in instruction manuals, with games, in recipe books. An example of a child's procedural writing is given in Figure 3.7 and an example of a published procedure in Figure 3.8.

Object of Game The object of the game is to get to the finish with all of the items.	GOAL
Equipment For the game you will need 1 dice 2–4 counters the 15 item cards.	MATERIALS AND EQUIPMENT
How to Play 1. Each player chooses a counter and the person who throws a six first starts. 2. After you have thrown the dice move the number spaces it says on it. 3. If you land on a shop pick up one item card if not carry on. If you land on a space which says lose something place the item it says in the lost item space. 4. If you have not got all the cards by the time you have got to the finish keep going round until you have got them. This game is for two-four players.	STEPS TO ACHIEVE THE GOAL
Sarah – Year 5	

Figure 3.7. Child's procedural writing.

Fire safety	GOAL
If you discover a fire 1 Operate the nearest Fire Alarm call point. 2 Call the Fire Brigade (9-999) on University Exchange giving the following address: 　School of Education (St Luke's), Heavitree Road, Exeter. 3 Report location of fire to the Head Porter/Duty Porter (Extn 4884). 4 Attack the fire if possible with an appliance provided, without taking personal risk or, 5 leave the building by the nearest available escape route and report the location of the fire to Officer i/c Fire Brigade. On hearing the alarm (a continuous ringing bell) 1 Leave the building by the nearest available escape route, closing doors behind. DO NOT return to collect personal belongings. 2 Proceed to your assembly point. DO NOT return to the building until informed it is safe to do so by the Officer i/c Fire Brigade.	STEPS TO ACHIEVE THE GOAL

Figure 3.8. Example of a procedural text. From: Fire instructions displayed in the corridors, University of Exeter, 1995.

PERSUASION GENRE

THE PURPOSE OF PERSUASIVE WRITING

Persuasive writing takes many forms from advertising copy to polemic pamphlets, but its purpose is always to promote one particular point of view or argument – unlike a discussion paper, which considers alternative points of view.

THE GENERIC STRUCTURE OF PERSUASION

A piece of persuasive writing usually consists of:

✦ an opening statement (the thesis, often in the form of position/preview)

> Fox hunting should be banned for it is a cruel and barbaric sport.

✦ the arguments (often in the form of point + elaboration)

> Foxes rarely attack domestic animals. Statistics show that ...

✦ a summary and re-statement of the opening position (reiteration)

> We have seen that...

Therefore, all the evidence points unmistakably to the conclusion that fox hunting is cruel and unnecessary.

THE LANGUAGE FEATURES OF PERSUASION

Persuasive text is usually written:

✦ in the simple present tense

> statistics show, it is

✦ focusing mainly on generic human participants

> hunters believe, environmentalists argue

✦ using mostly causal rather than temporal connectives.

> this shows, however, because

The persuasive genre is found in the literature produced by special interest groups, in political writing and in publicity and promotional material. An example of a child's persuasive writing is given in Figure 3.9 and an example of published persuasive writing in Figure 3.10.

I think that building houses on the old school field is a bad thing. I have several reasons for thinking this like the wildlife and the youth club.	POSITION PREVIEW	THESIS
My first reason is that it would be destroying wildlife on the field because of all the digging and when the people move in the noise, the light and other things.	POINT ELABORATION	ARGUMENTS
A further reason is the Youth club would not like it because they use the field for games and other things. And they might disturb the people in the houses.	POINT ELABORATION	
Furthermore there are enough houses in the village. We do not need anymore. It would just be a waste of space (We need that space)	POINT ELABORATION	
Therefore although some people think it would be a good thing to because it would create more homes I think I have shown lots of reasons why it is not a very good idea to build more houses here especially on the old school field	REITERATION	
James – Year 5		

Figure 3.9. Child's persuasive argument writing.

WELCOME TO Ways with Words at *THE ROYAL CRESCENT HOTEL*, Bath. *A LITERARY LUNCH with DENIS HEALEY:* *Sunday 27th November 1994* *A LITERARY BREAK : Sunday 26th – Tuesday* *28th February 1995* *If in the middle of dark, damp winter days you feel* *in need of a special treat a literary break at the* *Royal Crescent Hotel should prove a superb tonic.*	**THESIS**
The hotel offers a luxurious environment with great care given to every detail to make you feel comfortable. For residents on our literary break the days start with an extensive breakfast buffet in the lovely Dower House restaurant overlooking the garden and ends with a chocolate laid out on their pillows in one of the beautiful bedrooms. In between there are stimulating and intimate literary events in The Pavilion and literary dinners with first rate food and eminent guest speakers. At each event writers give talks and interviews about their work and their lives. There is an opportunity to ask questions and afterwards to buy books and get them signed by the writer if you wish.	**ARGUMENTS**
The chance to meet like-minded companions and relax in such a special hotel made our Royal Crescent events very popular last year.	**REITERATION**

Figure 3.10. Example of a persuasive text. Part of the booking leaflet for 'Ways with Words' Literary Weekends, 1995.

DISCUSSION GENRE

THE PURPOSE OF DISCUSSION

Discussion papers present arguments and information from differing viewpoints before reaching a conclusion based on the evidence.

THE GENERIC STRUCTURE OF DISCUSSION

A discussion paper usually consists of:

+ a statement of the issue and a preview of the main arguments

> Our school is trying to decide whether to have a uniform. Some people think it would improve the school while other groups argue that it is unnecessary and would stop our freedom of choice.

+ arguments for, with supporting evidence

> Children from our school look scruffy when compared to most of the other local schools who already have a uniform.

+ arguments against, with supporting evidence

> Most of the pupils believe very strongly that not wearing uniform allows them to feel more individual and grown-up because everybody looks the same in uniform. A recent poll held in the school showed that 90 per cent of pupils agreed that wearing their own clothes allowed them to express their identity.

+ recommendation given as a summary and conclusion

> One group wants to unify the school while the other group claims freedom of choice... I think...

The order of the arguments for and against can be reversed and it is worth considering which case you would want to present last and why. An alternative structure would be to present the argument and the counter-argument for each point at a time.

THE LANGUAGE FEATURES OF DISCUSSION TEXTS

Discussion is usually written:

+ in the simple present tense

> *look, feel*

The issue I would like to discuss is whether smoking is bad for you. Some people think that it is alright to smoke but other people say that it is bad for your health.	**STATEMENT OF ISSUE PREVIEW**
Some people think that smoking is enjoyable. They like having cigarettes. They say it gives you cool looks and that it helps you to concentrate on things better.	**ARGUMENTS FOR**
Children think it is cool when they see their friends and parents smoke and they see children on films and T.V. programmes smoking. Children smoke so that they look older and so they can get into pubs and clubs. Other people think that it gives you heart disease and lung cancer, and it damages your health. When a lady is pregnant, it could kill her baby.	**ARGUMENTS AGAINST**
Smoking makes you smell horrible and some people say it can lead to drugs. It is a habit you can't get out of and it's a waste of money. If people fall asleep when they are smoking it could cause a fire. I think that because there are more arguments against it is better not to smoke.	**RECOMMENDATION**
Laura – Year 6	

Figure 3.11. Child's discussion writing

ANTARCTICA – TO MIND IT OR TO MINE IT?	STATEMENT OF ISSUE
ENVIRONMENTALISTS ARGUE THAT: • *Mining always changes an environment in a big way. In Antarctica even small changes would destroy wildlife.* • *Accidents, such as oil spills, are certain to happen.* • *Like a freezer, the Antarctic weather stops waste breaking down. Waste disturbs wildlife breeding areas.* • *Antarctica should be a world park. The land, and the sea around it, should be left as a wilderness.* • *Antarctica should be a place of peace. People may fight over territory if they mine it.*	ARGUMENTS AGAINST MINING
MINING COMPANIES ARGUE THAT: • *Antarctica has a lot of oil and other minerals. People need these resources.* • *Mining companies could be told to obey strict safety rules. They could prevent accidents.* • *Mining companies could remove their waste.* • *Mining companies could do research that would help the world.* • *Countries who have an interest in Antarctica have signed a treaty. They are already working together peacefully.*	ARGUMENTS FOR MINING
WHAT DO YOU SAY? *MIND IT?* *OR* *MINE IT?*	RECOMMEND-ATION

Figure 3.12. Example of a discussion text. From: Issues *by R.Martin (Magic Bean series, Heinemann, 1991).*

+ using generic human (or non-human participants) rather than 'I' (except in the thesis/conclusion)

> pupils, children

+ using causal connectives

> therefore, because, etc.

The discussion genre is often found in philosophical texts, history and social studies texts and newspaper editorials. An example of a child's discussion is given in Figure 3.11 and an example of a published discussion in Figure 3.12.

Now you have looked at the differing generic structures and language features of the main non-fiction texts we would like to remind you of the question we raised in Chapter 2 – which kind of non-fiction writing do our pupils produce most frequently in the primary classroom? You have probably realised that it is *recount* writing. We often ask children to write recounts telling us about visits, events in their lives etc. They write recounts across the curriculum – in retelling historical events, in writing up science experiments or in detailing how they arrived at a solution in a maths problem-solving exercise. Recount writing is important but we need also to ensure that our children write in other forms. It may be interesting for you to look through the non-fiction writing your pupils have undertaken this term and see if recount writing does indeed dominate their writing repertoire.

SUMMARY

With the knowledge and vocabulary provided by this analysis of generic structures and their language features, we become able to discuss types of non-fiction texts with our pupils in the same way as we discuss narrative forms with them. Of course, not all texts will be in a single 'pure' form. Some may well contain a mixture of genres. For example, reports often contain a section which is an explanation, or a discussion may have elements of a report embedded within it. It is important to remember that real non-fiction texts are not always going to conform perfectly to one of the descriptions above. The analysis gives general guiding principles but, just as skilled writers play around with the story genre – perhaps starting with the ending, or deliberately writing a story in a non-fiction genre such as a mock police report – so non-fiction genres can be mixed, played around with, parodied. The generic structures are presented as an aid to understanding, not as a set of strait-jackets.

Furthermore we would caution against moving into formal lessons with children on text types and structures. We will discuss this issue in more detail in Chapter 4. Rather, knowledge about the different genres should be used to ensure that classrooms contain a full range of non-fiction texts. Our children should experience books, pamphlets, letters and documents of all kinds, written in a variety of genres. We need to read aloud to children from this wide range of non-fiction as well as from fiction, in order to help them become familiar with the structures, patterns and rhythms of all texts. This 'immersion' is important. What Margaret Meek (1988) says is as important for non-fiction as it is for fiction:

> The most important single lesson the children learn from texts is the nature and variety of written discourse, the different way that language lets a writer tell, and the many different ways a reader reads. (Page 21)

In Chapter 4 we will consider why it is important that children use these genres and how writing frames can help.

CHAPTER 4

THE WHY, WHEN AND HOW OF WRITING FRAMES

THE LANGUAGE OF POWER

Imagine you are the inspector appointed to review the proposed route of a new road. You have invited written evidence and receive a great many letters from the general public, all wishing to put forward arguments in favour of or against the road. Some letters make their case clearly – setting out and elaborating on each point before moving on to the next and ending with a summary. Others, although obviously deeply felt, are rambling and at times incoherent, and leave you with no clear idea of the points being argued or the evidence to support them. Which letters are you more likely to take into account when making your decision?

This imaginary situation is just an example of the importance in our society of being competent in writing non-fiction. Report, explanation, persuasion and discussion are powerful forms of language that we use to get things done. They are the language of governments and bureaucrats, public institutions and educational establishments. They have been called the 'language of power' (Kress, 1987) and it can be argued that pupils who leave our classrooms unable to use these genres are denied the means of becoming fully functioning members of society. One development programme in which a knowledge of the main non-fiction genres is being deliberately introduced into schools is called the 'Language and Social Power Project' and is part of the Disadvantaged Schools Project of New South Wales, Australia (Department of Employment, Education and Training, 1989).

Some linguists have claimed that in ensuring that our pupils have access to the whole range of non-fiction genres and that they can use them effectively, we are 'empowering' them to take part in a democratic society. This approach has been criticised as naive, and the counter-argument is put that simply having access to certain written forms does little to increase one's actual power in society. Barrs (1991/92), for example, wonders what difference it makes to the unemployed or to shop-floor workers that they can write a memo.

> Genres themselves are not powerful. It is indeed the 'possibility of their use' that counts most. It is not only knowing how to write that matters in this world but being in a position to ensure that your writing reaches an audience, and then that it is noticed or read. We could all learn how to write certain powerful genres – such as high level memos – but this would not increase our access to power by one jot (Barrs, page 12).

This is indeed true. Clearly we do not gain entry to the power bases of society just because we can read and write. Using non-fiction genres cannot in itself *empower* but it can *enable* citizens to function more effectively within society. The unemployed or shop-floor workers need to be able to communicate as effectively as the manager.

Over the past thirty years or so, much attention has been focused on encouraging children to write from personal experience and this has led to a revolution in the way writing has been approached. The process approach has undoubtedly encouraged children to write more freely and enthusiastically, but we must be alert to the possibility that children will continue to use a personal mode in much of their writing across the curriculum. They will often write up a science experiment or a procedure as an account of what they did. Kim's writing (Figure 4.1) is a clear example of this. The children in this Year 2 class had sown cress seeds and were then making their own seed packets in which to take some seeds home to sow at a later date. They had looked at some examples of seed packets and discussed the kind of information that was written on the back of them and the ways in which it was written. Kim wrote a straightforward recount.

Figure 4.1. Kim's seed packet 'instructions'.

Robert, who worked on the activity alongside Kim, recognised the appropriate genre and produced a procedural text (Figure 4.2).

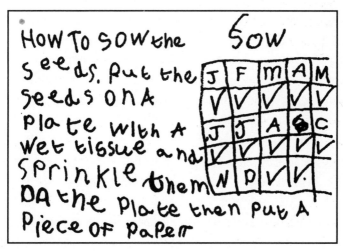

Figure 4.2. Robert's seed packet instructions.
'Over them' was written on the reverse of the paper and lost when the instructions were stuck on an envelope.

It could be argued that there were several reasons for the difference in form between Kim's and Robert's texts. Maybe they had different audiences and purposes in mind when they wrote. Certainly they had brought different experiences and expertise to the classroom and to the task. However, in this case, the children had been asked to write the instructions they would need to follow when they took the seeds home. It would seem that Kim lacked the experience of and/or failed to recognise the appropriate generic form that would have made her writing achieve its aim.

Some children, such as Robert, who is a competent language user, do move into using some non-fiction forms, because they have become familiar with these forms in their classrooms and the wider world. Indeed, it would seem from our work in classrooms that the procedural form is one that many children pick up naturally. It is one they are aware of from, for instance, the sets of rules that accompany games, the simple recipes they try out, the school fire drill notices, instructions on their classroom wall telling them how to use the computer, and the instructions in the photo booth in the town centre. Of course, such 'natural' learning is not simply a process of osmosis. Learning is an active, constructive and social process. Margaret Meek (1988) among others has shown us that many of the 'untaught' lessons that children pick up are learned from books – through reading and being read to. We have already mentioned the importance of teachers immersing children in as wide a range of different genres as possible, through reading aloud and discussion.

For Robert, the 'untaught' lessons have clearly been fruitful and yet, within any class of children, there will be many who continue to use the personal recount for much of their non-fiction writing, in spite of being offered examples of different genres and given purposeful opportunities to practise them. As important as story and expressive writing are, it is also crucial that we introduce children to more impersonal forms; and writing frames are one way of helping some children become familiar with particular non-fiction genres. The strategy is to use the writing frames to help children practise the generic structures of recount, report, procedure, explanation, persuasion and discussion, until they have assimilated these forms into their own writing repertoire.

WHAT ARE WRITING FRAMES?

Writing frames are outline structures, enabling children to produce non-fiction writing in the different generic forms. Given these structures or skeleton outlines of starters, connectives and sentence modifiers, children can concentrate on communicating what they want to say. As they practise building their writing around the frames, they become increasingly familiar with the generic forms.

The work of Cairney (1990) on story frames and Cudd and Roberts (1989) on 'expository paragraph frames' first suggested to us the value there might be in giving children structures around which to build their early non-fiction writing. Cairney described story frames as 'a form of probed text recall' and a 'story level cloze', while Cudd and Roberts claimed that expository frames 'provide a bridge which helps ease the transition from narrative to content area reading and writing'. Cudd and Roberts' frames, however, were largely in recount genre. We were concerned to introduce children to a wider variety of genres. As a result, in collaboration with teachers, we have developed a range of writing frames for use in the classroom. The frames have been widely used throughout the primary and lower secondary years, with children of all abilities, including children with special needs. On the strength of this extensive trialling we are reasonably confident in saying that writing frames not only help children become familiar with unfamiliar genres, but also help overcome many of the other problems often associated with non-fiction writing.

HOW WRITING FRAMES HELP WITH THE PROBLEMS OF WRITING NON-FICTION

A reason often given for some of the difficulties which children experience in writing non-fiction is that they are sometimes unsure about the differences between speech and written language. Bereiter and Scardamalia (1985) point out the supportive nature of conversation: people take turns to speak, each prompting someone else to say something. This helpful prompting is missing from the relationship between a writer and a blank sheet of paper. Bereiter and Scardamalia's research has shown that a teacher's oral promptings during writing can extend a child's written work, with no drop in quality. The prompts act as an 'external trigger of discourse production' (page 97). Bereiter and Scardamalia suggest that children need to 'acquire a functional substitute for... an encouraging listener.' We believe that the written prompts provided by writing frames help children move from relying on the teacher's oral promptings to writing independently.

Other problems often mentioned in connection with children's reading and writing of non-fiction are the complexity of the cohesive ties children have to recognise and use, the use of more formal registers, and the use of technical vocabulary (Halliday and Hasan, 1976; Perera, 1984; Anderson and Armbruster, 1981; Littlefair, 1991). In the following text, for example, we can see the complex cohesive ties that a child would need to recognise in order to identify who 'they' refers to. The many technical words and the use of the formal third person are both features which may be unfamiliar and thus confusing.

> For thousands of years, scientists and technologists have been able to make new substances from old ones. We are not sure when people first learned how to get metals out of the Earth's rocks, but we do know that some of them were quite good at it five thousand years ago. That was in the part of the world we now call Iraq. They got the metals copper and tin from local rocks and mixed them together to

make a new, very useful metal called bronze.

The Egyptians made iron from iron ore four thousand five hundred years ago, and about a thousand years later they made glass from sand and a substance called soda.

To make these substances, *they* [our italics] needed some observations, some luck, and lots of pattern statements. They worked out ways of getting the substances they needed. But they weren't very good at explaining why the methods worked.

(*How Scientists Work.* Pupil's Book 1, page 70, Nuffield Science 11–13, Longman, 1989)

Again we believe that writing frames can serve to familiarise children with the use of these difficult features. The frames help to maintain the cohesion of the whole, provide appropriate connectives, model the more formal register of much non-fiction writing and introduce more technical vocabulary.

TEACHER MODELLING AND SHARED WRITING

The first stage in the introduction of writing frames should, we believe, be based on teacher modelling and shared or joint writing.

Vygotsky (1978) proposed the idea that children first experience a particular cognitive activity in collaboration with expert practitioners. The child begins as a spectator, as the majority of the cognitive work is done by the expert (usually a parent or a teacher). Then he or she becomes a novice, taking over some of the work under the close supervision of the expert. As the child grows in experience and capability of performing the task, the expert hands over greater and greater responsibility but still acts as a guide, assisting the child at problematic points. Eventually, the child assumes full responsibility for the task with the expert still present in the role of a supportive audience. This model, shown diagrammatically in Figure 4.3, fits established theories about teaching and learning. It is also a model which is familiar to teachers who have adopted such teaching strategies as paired reading and an apprenticeship approach.

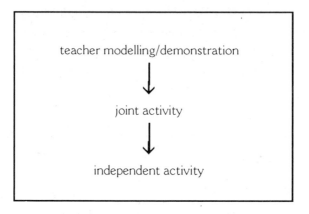

Figure 4.3

TEACHER MODELLING IN PRACTICE

Ms L. wanted to introduce some of her more able Year 2 children to procedural writing, by giving them a genuine reason to produce texts in this genre. The class at the time was doing a topic on toys. The children were constructing a series of small toys, including many of the usual simple moving ones, such as whirlers, spinners and message papers with lift-up flaps. These simple toys were to provide preliminary experience before the class moved on to make more complex moving things. One group had made message toys and Ms L. told them that together they were now going to write a set of instructions which the rest of the class could use when their turn came to make this kind of toy. Ms L. began by modelling how to write a procedure. She conducted a shared writing session using a large sheet of sugar paper on an easel. During this session she and the children wrote alternately. After working with the group to compose the title (goal) and the list of materials that were needed, Ms L. provided the first sentence of the instructions. This was in the imperative (see Figure 4.4).

How to make a moving message toy
You need: a square piece of paper
a pencil and crayons
1. Fold the paper in half into a triangle shape.
2. Fold it again into triangles.
3. Open it back into a square.
4. We folded each corner into the middle.
5. Turn it over.
6. Turn each corner into the middle again.
7. Put your fingers in the flaps on the underneath side
and bend the toy into the right shape. This is hard so
ask someone who's done it.
8. Put a different colour dot on each flap and write a
message underneath the flap.
9. Play with it with your friends.
10. Don't play with it in class or the teacher
will be cross.

Figure 4.4. Shared writing of a procedural text.

This sentence, 'Fold the paper in half into a triangle shape', provided a model of the register needed for the rest of the instructions, which the children were invited to provide. Two more steps were offered and written, both maintaining the imperative, procedural form. At step 4, however, one child offered and then wrote: 'We folded each corner into the middle.' This child had slipped into recount genre: Ms L. then read out the whole piece of writing to date to the children and asked for their comments. Sasha said: 'That's not the right kind of sentence.' Ms L. asked the rest of the group if they agreed and if so what was wrong with the sentence. They were able to point out that none of the other sentences contained the word 'we' and that all the 'right kind of sentences told you what to do'. Ms L. then asked how sentence 4 could be made into the right kind of sentence. 'We' was crossed out and discussion followed as to whether the sentence was now 'right'. Changing 'folded' into 'fold' was soon suggested and the group was happy that the sentence finally conformed to the rest of the text. Ms L. was then able to introduce a short discussion on the past and the imperative tenses.

Notice how, in this example, the children had a real reason for writing in the procedural genre. The modelling of the form arose within the context of their on-going work and normal writing practice. After several shared writing sessions using this genre, most of the children in the class began to use it independently. However, there were still a few who continued to write recounts or pieces that were a mixture of recount and procedure (see Figure 4.5).

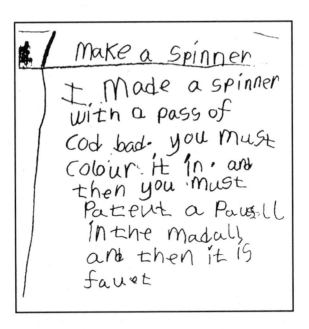

Figure 4.5. Mixed recount and procedural writing. Year 2.

This suggests that there are some children for whom teacher modelling does not work so successfully, especially in busy, over-populated classrooms. This method of teaching is constructed around an ideal of a child and an expert working together one-to-one which is rarely feasible, of course. In particular, it seems that children are too often expected to move into the independent writing phase before they are really ready and often the pressure put on them to do so is a result of the practical problem that teachers do not have the time to give the children individual support. What is clearly needed is something to bridge the gap between the joint activity phase and the independent activity phase.

We have called this additional phase the *scaffolded phase* – a phase where we offer our pupils strategies to aid writing, but strategies that they can use without an adult necessarily being alongside them (see Figure 4.6). Writing frames are one such strategy.

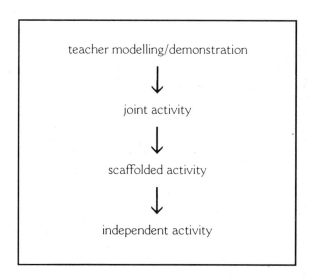

Figure 4.6.

HOW TO USE THE FRAMES

Discussion and teacher modelling should always be the first stages in using a frame, followed by joint construction (teacher and child/ren together) before each child undertakes his or her own writing supported by the frame. This discussion, teacher modelling, joint construction pattern of teaching is vital, for it not only introduces the generic form and teaches the words that signal connections and transitions but also provides opportunities for developing children's oral language and their thinking. Some children, especially those with learning difficulties, may need many oral sessions and sessions in which their teacher acts as a scribe before they are ready to attempt their own framed writing.

It is useful to make big versions of the frames for the teacher modelling and joint construction phases. These large frames can be used for shared writing. It is important that the child and the teacher understand that the frame is a supportive draft and that words on it may be crossed out or substituted. Extra sentences may be added or surplus starters deleted. The frame should be treated as a flexible aid, not a rigid form.

WHEN TO USE THE FRAMES

We are convinced that practising writing in a range of genres is most effective if it is done in the context of meaningful experiences. The concept of 'situated learning' (Lave and Wenger, 1991) suggests that learning is always context-dependent. For this reason, we have *always* used the frames within class topic work rather than in isolated study-skills lessons (Lewis, Wray and Rospigliosi, 1995). British primary school teaching is still largely based on this model of curriculum planning and we would argue very strongly for its potential effectiveness.

We do *NOT* advocate using the frames for the direct teaching of generic structures in skills-centred lessons. *The frame itself is never a reason for writing.* There is much questioning of the appropriateness of the direct teaching of generic forms (for example, Barrs, 1991/92; Cairney, 1992) and we share many of the reservations expressed by such commentators. Our use of a writing frame has always arisen from a child having a *purpose* for undertaking some writing. The appropriate frame has been introduced to give the child extra help.

You may decide to offer children the help of a frame in the following situations.

✦ When they first attempt independent writing in an unfamiliar genre.

✦ When they appear to be stuck in a particular mode of writing, for example, constantly using 'and then' when writing an account.

✦ When they 'wander' between genres in a way that demonstrates a lack of understanding of the way a particular genre is used. For instance, when writing a procedural text such as a recipe a child may start in a second person/instructional mode ('First you beat the egg') but then shift into a recount ('Next I stirred in the flour'). Mixing genres can, of course, be deliberate and creative. We must take care to differentiate between occasions when a child purposely moves between genres and those where different genres are confused.

✦ When they have used one genre (often a personal recount) to write something (for instance, a science experiment) which would be more appropriate in a different genre. Although writing accounts from personal experience is a vital part of the process of becoming a writer (cf Britton's work on the expressive mode), we must judge when a child needs help in adopting other genres. The National Curriculum English document (DES, 1990) states that children must 'produce a range of types of non-chronological writing' (Attainment Target 3 Level 3d).

We would stress that, in all of these situations, writing frames are just one of a range of strategies and writing experiences that a teacher would offer to assist the children.

USING THE FRAMES WITH A RANGE OF WRITERS

We have found the frames helpful to children of all ages and all abilities. Their wide applicability is one of their most positive features. They have been used with children from Key Stage 1 to Key Stage 4. However, teachers have found the frames particularly useful with children of average writing ability, with those who find writing difficult and with children with special needs in literacy. Teachers have commented on the improved quality (and quantity) of writing that has resulted from using the frames with these children.

It would, of course, be unnecessary to use a frame with writers already confident and fluent in a particular genre, but frames can be used to introduce such writers to new genres. Teachers have noted an initial dip in quality when comparing the framed 'new genre' writing with the fluent recount writing of an able child. However, they have then discovered that, after only a few uses of a frame, that able child adds the new genre and its language features into his or her repertoire and produces fluent writing of high quality in that genre too.

The aim with all children is for them to reach this stage of assimilating the generic structures and language features into their own writing repertoires. Writing frames should be used with a particular child or with a small group of children, as and when they need them. They are not intended as class worksheets, for within any class there will always be children who do not need them.

In the next chapter we will look at examples of the frames in classroom usage. Then, in the concluding chapter, we will examine how the language features of genres can be discussed and developed with children, and when to stop using frames.

THE FRAMES IN USE: RECOUNT, REPORT, PROCEDURE, EXPLANATION, PERSUASIVE ARGUMENT, DISCUSSION

In this chapter we will look at examples of the writing frames and how they have been used in the classroom. In every case the frames have been used within the context of on-going classroom work, when an opportunity arose to write in a particular genre. Always, work began with teacher demonstration or shared writing. The examples included are of shared framed writing as well as of individual children's work.

USING RECOUNT FRAMES

Most children already write many recounts and have an unspoken knowledge of this generic form. The genre is important and familiar. Therefore frames are most useful for offering alternative starters and connectives and encouraging children to write more extended and thoughtful pieces.

THE 'PRIOR KNOWLEDGE + REACTION' AND THE 'PRIOR KNOWLEDGE + REVISION' FRAMES

These frames encourage children to base their accounts on what they have *learned* rather than what they *did*. This shift in focus moves children away from a straight chronological recount towards one that is more reflective. The frames begin by asking pupils to think about what they already know about a topic. There is now a great deal of research which indicates the importance of children's prior knowledge in their understanding of new information (Anderson and Pearson, 1984; Anderson, 1977). Furthermore, it appears that, if it is to be useful, this prior knowledge needs to be brought to the forefront of the learner's mind, that is, made explicit (Bransford, 1983). Schema theory suggests that our brains do not contain a random collection of items of knowledge but that our knowledge is structured and categorised into schema — organised cognitive 'maps' of the parts of the world we know about. The concepts that constitute a schema are said to 'provide slots that can be instantiated with specific information.' (Wilson and Anderson, 1986, page 33). When we encounter new information we incorporate it into our existing schema either by accretion (adding detail to the map) or restructuring (altering the map to fit the new information). The two writing frames given here follow the pattern of accretion (Figure 5.1) and restructuring (Figure 5.2).

Although I already knew that
I have learned some new facts
I learned that
I also learned
Another fact I learned was
However, the most interesting thing I learned was

Figure 5.1. Prior knowledge + reactions (accretion model).

Before I began this topic I thought that
but when I read about it I found out
I also learned
Another fact I learned was
Finally I learned

Figure 5.2. Prior knowledge + revision frame
(restructuring model).

Focusing on the children's prior knowledge gives them an active role in the writing right from the beginning. Asking them what they know enhances their self-esteem and sense of 'ownership' of knowledge. The *prior knowledge + reaction frame* (Figures 5.1 and 5.3) not only allows children to pass some comment on what seems of particular significance to them within a topic but also offers a model of how to build some excitement into a piece of writing. By keeping the 'most interesting' item until the end, the piece concludes with a strong 'punch line'. The reader is 'invited' to reassess the previous facts mentioned in the light of this final significant one.

The *prior knowledge + revision frame* (Figures 5.2 and 5.4) helps children to reflect on anything they have discovered which conflicts with what they already knew. It can be quite difficult to get children to acknowledge their misconceptions and change their views about the world. They will often ignore information that contradicts what they think they know already. This frame shows them that it is permissible to change your mind in the light of fresh evidence.

Use of the frames should always begin with discussion and teacher modelling, as described in Chapter 4. One group of children, for example, had collected pages of directly copied notes in their jotters as part of a topic on 'Underground'. They were asked to talk about one thing that they had found during their research which had made them think, 'Oh, that's really interesting. I didn't know that', or about any discovery that had made them change their minds about the subject. After a lively discussion, *a prior knowledge + reaction frame* and a *prior knowledge + revision frame* were introduced. The teacher had prepared two big frames which she used to show how the information could be written up. The children were then asked to select one of the frames to guide their own writing. It was stressed that the frames could be altered by the writer. For example, 'when I read about it' might be 'when I saw it 'or 'when I visited it'. The writing produced by two of the group is given in Figures 5.3 and 5.4.

Oil Rigs

Although I already knew that
oil is produced by oil rigs
that are stationed in the middle of
seas and oceans and drill about 30 metres
deep to reach the oil,

I have learnt some new facts.
I learnt that a part of the rig
called the drill string could weigh
up to hundreds of tonnes.

I also learnt that
is the people on the oilrig get
bored they could go and watch the
cinema on the oil rig

A nother fact I learnt is they used
mini submarines and some wear speacil
suits so they can dive deeper than scuba
divers

However the most intresting thing I
learnt was that oil rigs take 800
tonnes of paint to paint the whole rig

Figure 5.3. Prior knowledge + reaction frame.
Richard – Year 4.

Before I began this topic I thought that the male rabbits where the ones who dug the warrens. But when I red about it. I found out that it was actual the females who did all the work, as usual!

I also learnt that the passages or burrows are up to 3m long and 15 cm wide so the rabbits can get though easily.

Secondly I learnt that the warren can be over 80 years old and around 30 rabbits can live in one.

Finally I learnt that the rabbits warren has lots of ways in and out, so if one is blocked a rabbit can get in another.

Also a warren is only for one family.

Figure 5.4. Prior knowledge + revision frame. Mary – Year 4.

These children had now conveyed their own interpretation of information they had previously just copied. The personalised sentence structures of the writing frames helped greatly in encouraging the children to move away from parroting text towards using their own voice.

USING PRIOR KNOWLEDGE + REACTION FRAMES FOR SELF-ASSESSMENT

There is also an element of self-assessment in the *prior knowledge + reaction frame* and, if the final phrase becomes 'However, the most *important* thing I learned was...', the frame can be used at the end of a unit of work. Figure 5.5 shows the frame in use by a university student at the end of a course unit.

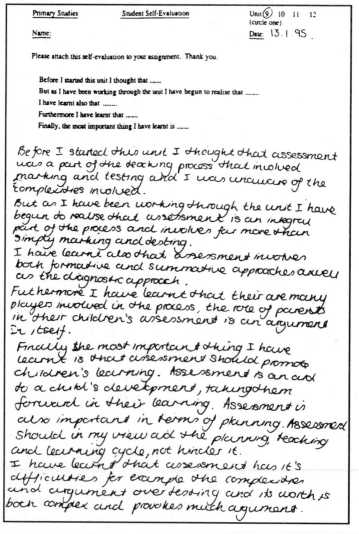

Figure 5.5. Prior knowledge + reaction frame used as a student self-assessment guide.

PRIOR KNOWLEDGE + REACTION AND PRIOR KNOWLEDGE + REVISION VISIT FRAMES

Most teachers will be familiar with the kind of writing children often produce after a school trip. Much of it can be described as 'bed to bed retelling', because it consists of a simple recounting of the events of the day. For example: 'I got up and had my breakfast ... then I went to school. We went on a trip to ... On the coach we ate our sandwiches ... In the shop I bought ... then we went back to school ...'. This is greeted by teachers almost universally with dismay.

Using a frame can transform this writing into a personalised, detailed account of what has been *learned*. See Figures 5.6 and 5.7. In both of these examples, written after visits to museums, the children have concentrated on the new knowledge they have acquired. The writing remains an individual personal reflection on the visit, but has moved on from the chronological account of trivial details of the journey.

SEQUENTIAL FRAMES

Recounts are usually chronological. That is, events are described in the time sequence in which they took place, and this often means that children adopt an 'and then, and then, and then' mode of writing. The *sequential frame* offers alternatives to 'and then'. It also provides a logical structure, to help those children who find it hard to hold a sequence in their head. In the example of a child's work shown in Figure 5.8, the given frame consisted of those sentences and phrases not underlined. More connectives relating to time are suggested in the section on writing your own frames in Chapter 6.

ENUMERATION FRAMES

Listing is a genre familiar to most children at an early stage through shopping lists, Christmas lists, etc. The *enumeration frame* uses this well-known form within recount writing. Most children find it an easy structure to use. At the same time it allows them again to express a personal assessment of what

Are trip to Plymouth museum

Although I already knew that the Egyptian buried their dead in mummy cases it was nice seeing real one. They painted wonderful details picher on the mummy cases.

I have learnt some new facts. I learnt that the Egyptian put a littele statue of a scarab beettle next to the heart of a person when they died.

I also leamt that the Egyptians mummy fid their animals.

Another fact I leant was that they had lots of gods and they also worship all their gods too.

However the most interesting thing I learnt was that there was a god who listened to lies but if a Egyptian had a necklace of that god and if they rubbed the tummy of it the lie woun-t count.

Figure 5.6. Prior knowledge +
reaction visit frame. Year 5.

Dartmoor

Before I began this I thought that Dartmoor was just a place were it was peaceful and with wild life parks.

But when I visited it I found out that there were howres there in 4000 Bc.

I also Learnt that a boy called og made a very good water prof house in 4000 Bc.

Another fact I Learnt about Dartmoor is that the first letter box was hidden in cranmere pool.

Finally I Learnt that Dartmoor Rangers look after the park.   by Sarah

*Figure 5.7. Prior knowledge +
revision visit frame. Year 4.*

If a chick is to hatch out from a shell

First it must <u>stay in the shell togrou</u>

Next <u>the chick pecks the shell to break</u> <u>out</u>

Then <u>it hatches out of the egg</u> <u>and climbs out</u>

Finally <u>the feathers dry yellow</u> <u>and fluffy</u>

Now it is a chick

A newly hatched chick.

Figure 5.8. Sequential frame.
Year 2.

they have learned. Many teachers have used this frame to encourage children to look back and summarise their work at the end of a term (see Figure 5.9).

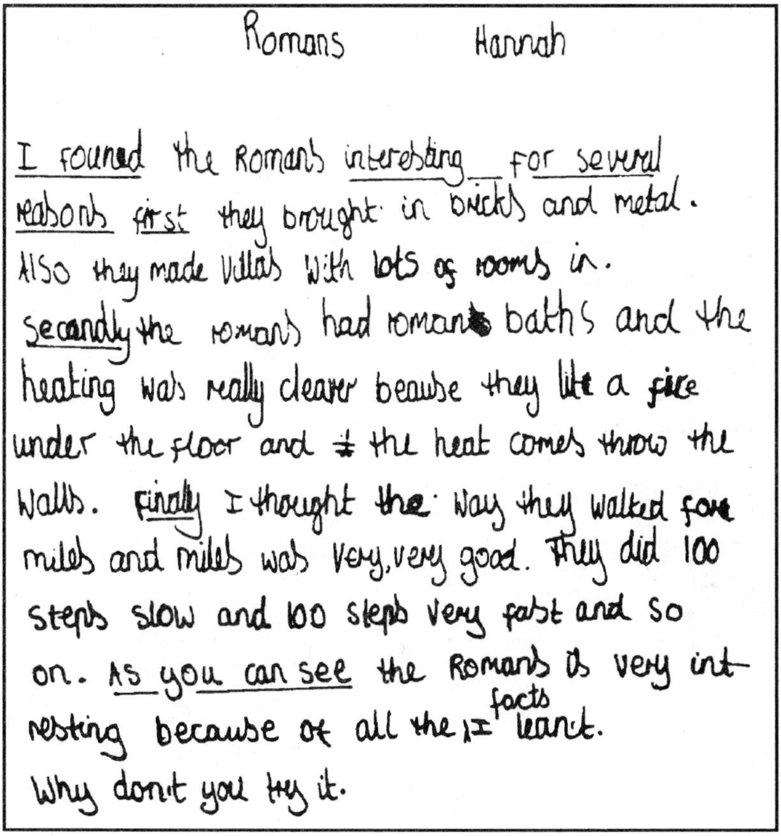

Romans   Hannah

I found the Romans interesting for several reasons first they brought in bricks and metal. Also they made villas with lots of rooms in. secondly the romans had romans baths and the heating was really cleaver beause they lit a fire under the floor and the heat comes throw the walls. finally I thought the way they walked for miles and miles was very, very good. They did 100 steps slow and 100 steps very fast and so on. As you can see the Romans is very interesting because of all the facts I learnt. Why don't you try it.

Figure 5.9. Enumeration frame.
Hannah – Year 5.

USING REPORT FRAMES

Reports usually start with a general classification, followed by descriptive details of the subject. Because the aspects to be described vary, depending on the subject being discussed, it proved difficult to provide just one generic frame that would cover all cases. It is preferable if frames are designed specially to suit particular report topics. For example, the frame shown in Figure 5.10 was designed to structure report writing on the topic of living things. As is the case throughout this book the precise structure given is only intended as a guide, to point teachers towards producing their own writing frames for specific occasions and specific children.

The report frame encourages children to start by placing the subject on which they are reporting into some kind of set or category. Different starters or headings can then be provided for the descriptive details that follow, to suit the individual report being written.

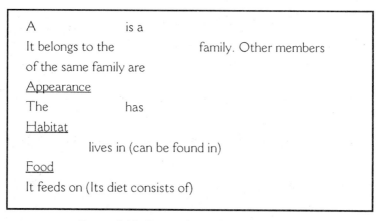

A   is a

It belongs to the   family. Other members

of the same family are

Appearance

The   has

Habitat

               lives in (can be found in)

Food

It feeds on (Its diet consists of)

Figure 5.10. Report frame for living things.

Report frames can be particularly useful when children have amassed a great deal of information on an object or living thing and need help in organising it into a whole. Jane's report on Viking houses (Figure 5.11), for example, would be more coherent, and thus a better piece of writing, if the details about each aspect of the house were grouped together. As it stands, descriptions of the fire and the materials used for building are jumbled. Figure 5.12 shows a similar piece of writing which has been 'framed' under various headings.

COMPARISON AND CONTRAST FRAMES

We often set children the task of comparing and contrasting objects. By asking them, for example, to compare a Victorian

Viking houses were made of wood
They had a hole for the smoke
to go out and the food was in
barrels. The floor had rushes
on it The roof was made
of Selaand they kept their food in
chests. The fire was in the
middle of the house and made the
house Smokey ~~The whe~~ They made
their house out of wood straw
and mud.

Figure 5.11. Unframed report. Jane – Year 3.

flat iron with a modern iron, we are encouraging them to use something they know as a 'hook' to which new knowledge can be attached. For comparing and contrasting, a version of the report genre is needed.

In a *comparison* or *contrast* frame (Figures 5.13 and 5.14), an opening classification brings together the objects in question. The opening statement of the frame in Figure 5.14, for example, might be completed: 'Although Birmingham and London are both large cities, they are different in many ways...'. This is followed by a description of the objects' similarities and differences.

Victorian Houses

Our town has lots of houses built about 100 years ago.

The type of house and the building materials

Most of the houses are terraced houses. There are some big detached houses which would have been for 1 family but are lots of flats now then

They are built of brick, some of the bricks are different colours are they are used to make patterns around the windows

The roofs have slate tiles and chimney pots.

The front doors are wood and some have stained glass

Lighting and heating

The houses had coal fires in victorian times and lots of the houses had pretty fire places with tiles at the sides. There was a coal shed in the back yard or else coal was tiped in the cellar. They had gas for lights on the wall or oil lamps or candles. Only rich people had gas.

Furniture

Rich Victorians had lots of wood furniture and ornaments. The chairs were very padded. The rooms were crowded and pianos were popular.

Poor people didn't have much furniture

Figure 5.12. A framed report. Year 5. The opening sentence of the report was constructed jointly by the teacher and the group using the frame. This is the child's final draft.

Although   and   are   different
they are alike in some interesting ways.
For example they both

They are also similar in that

The   is the same as

They also resemble each other in

Finally they both

Figure 5.13. A comparison report frame.

Although   and   are both
          they are different in many ways.
The   has   whilst   has

They are also different in that

Another way they in which they differ is

Finally

Figure 5.14. A contrast report frame.

Comparing and contrasting are sophisticated skills, for which most children will require support. Before they attempt to write using these frames, many children might benefit from setting out their information graphically, for example on a grid as shown in Figure 5.15.

	What I ate yesterday	What the Greeks ate
Breakfast	Nothing	bread & fruit or a lump of bread & soaked in wine.
Lunch	pasta and cheese & potatos	bread with a piece of cheese or some olives and figs.
Evening meal	Fish & chips bread & butter tomato sauce	vegetables fish meat bread.
Snacks	Apple crumble.	Pomegranetes
Drinks	Tango and water	water milk & wine.

Figure 5.15. Example of a grid used before writing a comparison report.

Using the grid encourages children to compare like with like, which they otherwise tend not to do. Look at the piece of writing in Figure 5.16. Before comparing this, Sarah had completed a comparison grid on the topic of Victorian and modern houses. She had also had a good deal of experience of using comparison writing frames. Her unframed writing seems to prove the value of the earlier practice. She not only compares similar aspects of houses, but also uses appropriate language to do so, as, for example, in 'Victorian houses *differ from...*' and '*Whilst* the Victorians had ...'.

USING PROCEDURAL FRAMES

Procedural frames can be used to guide the writing of any set of instructions. They support children's use of the more formal register. As we have seen, young children often write up procedures as recounts, and this may be a perfectly good response to being asked to write about what they have done. Such a request tends to invite a recount. If, however, the

A Comparison of a Middle-class Victorian home with a Modern home.

houses

Victorian houses differ from modern houses in the way that the Victorians had door bells pulled with a rope however we have electric bells. Whilst the Victorians had fancy doors most of us nowadays dont bother. Victorian people had flowers Because of this they used to decorate their houses with flower-painted tiles, This does not differ much from the modern fashion of decorating kitchens and bathrooms with floral tiles. The Victorians also used floral tiles to make their garden paths prettier, whilst modern homes dont do this. Victorian houses had big fire places and modern houses still do. Their walls had dado rails which stopped the furniture from rubbing against the wall paper. Churches have stained glass windows which differ from the windows used in houses.

Figure 5.16. Comparative report written by Sarah – Year ?,
who had had previous 'framed' experience of such writing.
This was written after first completing a grid.

purpose of a piece of writing is to instruct others in how to perform a task, a recount is clearly not the most effective genre. In our classroom work we found that children often came to understand the structural and linguistic features of procedural texts fairly rapidly and needed to use a frame on only one or two occasions. The experience of shared writing was also sufficient for many of them to realise the features of instructions.

Again, there are several versions of the procedural frame, each with its own vocabulary and layout, although following the same generic structure. (see Figures 5.17 and 5.18).

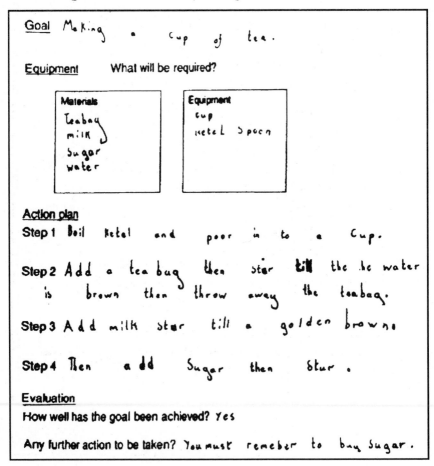

Figure 5.17. Procedural frame.
Year 9, special needs child.

How to make a cube out of a net

You will need: Card, wrapping paper, a pair of scissors, a pencil, a ruler and some glue.

1. First draw a net of a cube on your piece of card.

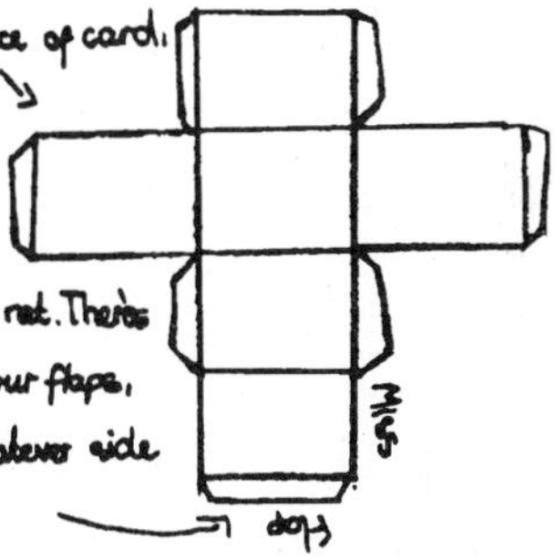

2. Then draw flaps on every other side of your net. There's a ryme that helps you workout where to put your flaps, its called Miss Flap. You say Miss Flap and whatever side "flap" lands on is where you draw the flap.

3. Next stick wrapping paper on the other side of your card.

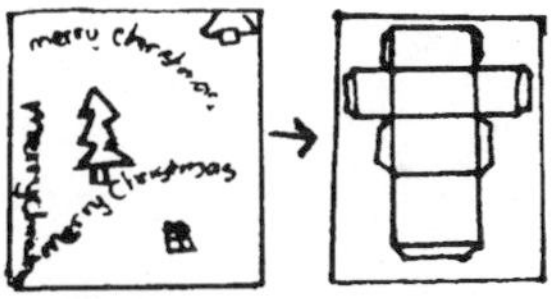

4. Cut out your net CAREFULLY, Remember NOT to cut off the flaps!

5. Score along the lines of your net with a ruler and scissors, crease and fold along the scored lines and your cube can be assembled!

6. Put the glue on the tabs and stick the tabs to the left hand side of each flap and wait for it to dry, and your cube is finished. Your finished cube.

by Amy

10/11/93

Figure 5.18. Procedural text. Amy – Year 4.
The given frame is underlined.

USING EXPLANATION FRAMES

When devising and trialling explanation frames we found that, as with report frames, one frame alone could not cover all the types of explanation that children might want to write. Continuing (as yet unpublished) work on writing genres in Australia has led to a proposal that explanation can be sub-divided further into three types: temporal, causal and factorial. This largely confirms what we discovered when trying to devise an explanation writing frame. There are different types of explanation and, although their generic structure is broadly the same, the language features they exhibit, in particular the connectives they employ, vary. Temporal explanations, for example, use connectives such as 'subsequently, 'eventually' and 'later', whereas causal explanations use connectives such as 'thus', 'as a result', 'therefore' and 'this causes'. Of course, some explanations contain a mixture of causal, temporal and factorial elements.

THE EXPLANATION FRAMES

Figure 5.19 shows a *causal/temporal frame*. Note that the connectives used may be unfamiliar to children to begin with, and this again reminds us that frames cannot be used 'cold'. Teacher modelling and shared writing are vital if the children are to understand the more formal vocabulary involved here.

```
I want to explain how/why
To begin with/It starts by
and this makes/means/changes/causes
After that
and as a result
Next
Then
The final result is that the
```

Figure 5.19. A mixed casual/temporal explanation frame.

Other explanation frames with which we have worked (see Figures 5.20 and 5.21) ask children to make some judgement about the several reasons which may make up an explanation, and to decide what 'the chief reason' is. This *factorial explanation frame* encourages children to think carefully before they write. Deciding which is the chief reason encourages lively debate and careful judgement of the information gathered.

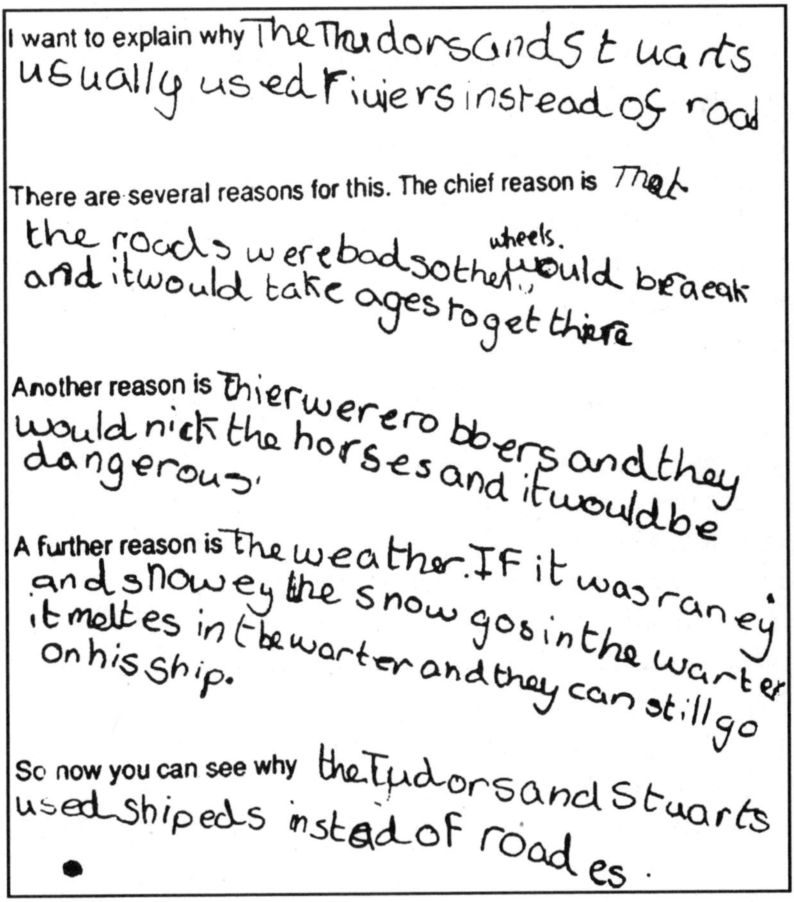

I want to explain why The Thudors and Stuarts usually used riviers instead of road

There are several reasons for this. The chief reason is That the roads were bad so the wheels. would beaeak and it would take ages to get there

Another reason is thier were robbers and they would nick the horses and it would be dangerous.

A further reason is the weather. If it was raney and snowey the snow gos in the warter it meltes in the warter and they can still go on his ship.

So now you can see why the Tudors and Stuarts used shipeds instad of roades.

Figure 5.20. Explanation written by a child with special needs, Year 5.

A further explanation frame (Figure 5.21) allows for the possibility of alternative views.

There are differing explanations as to why (how, what, when, etc)

One explanation is that

The evidence for this is

An alternative explanation is

This explanation is based on

Of the alternative explanations I think the most likely is

Figure 5.21. An explanation frame allowing for conflicting theories.

USING PERSUASIVE ARGUMENT FRAMES

As when using any of the frames given in this book, discussion, teacher modelling and shared construction of texts are vital first stages in introducing children to the writing of arguments. Many children will also find it helpful to give some kind of preliminary organisation to their ideas. Getting them to make a series of 'protest banners', each containing one statement that supports their main argument, allows them to record their ideas in a fairly unstructured way. They can then think about grouping their ideas together and begin to use a frame to help them with the coherence of their writing. Figure 5.22 shows the framed persuasive writing of a Year 7 child. The children in this class felt strongly about the issue of school uniform but notice how the child has written a well structured general argument (they think, they choose) to support her personal viewpoint.

As children become more experienced in arguing a case, the less support they need. Figure 5.23 shows an example of a reduced frame where the writer is merely given a list of connectives as a reminder of the type of cohesive phrases he or she might use.

One group of children we were working with decided for themselves that writing in this genre gave them a powerful way of expressing their feelings. The class had been moved from the main building of their school into a mobile classroom on the

Although not every body would agree, I want to argue that

> Children Should not wear school uniform.

I have several reasons for arguing for this point of view. My first reason is That they feel more comfortable in cl nes which they choose to wear.

> They would feel more relaxed and be able to work better and concentrate more on

A nother reason is their work.

> There wouldn't be the problem, of parents not wanting to buy school uniforms because they

Furthermore think they are too expensive. of too

> Some times you might wake up and find your two lots of uniform in the wash. cnps . . .'

Therefore, although some people argue that

> Children might take it past the limits.

I think I have shown that

> Children should be able to choose their clothing just as adults do, as long as they wear sensible clothes.

Figure 5.22. Persuasive writing. Year 6 child.

I would like to persuade you that	These words and phrases might help you.
	because
There are several points I want to make to support my point of view. Firstly	*therefore*
	you can see
	a supporting argument
	this shows that
	another piece of evidence is

Figure 5.23. Persuasive frame.

edge of the playground, and the children were finding that they were disturbed by the noise that other pupils made as they went past to games and to the hall. They made up their minds to mount a campaign to make the rest of the school aware of their problem. Some of them would produce a series of posters urging other children in the school to keep quiet when walking past the mobile classroom. Others planned to talk to the rest of the school during an assembly. There were several, however. who wanted to write to express their point of view. They felt that such pieces of writing, sent to each of the other classes, would allow them to put their case fully. An example of one of these pieces is given in Figure 5.24.

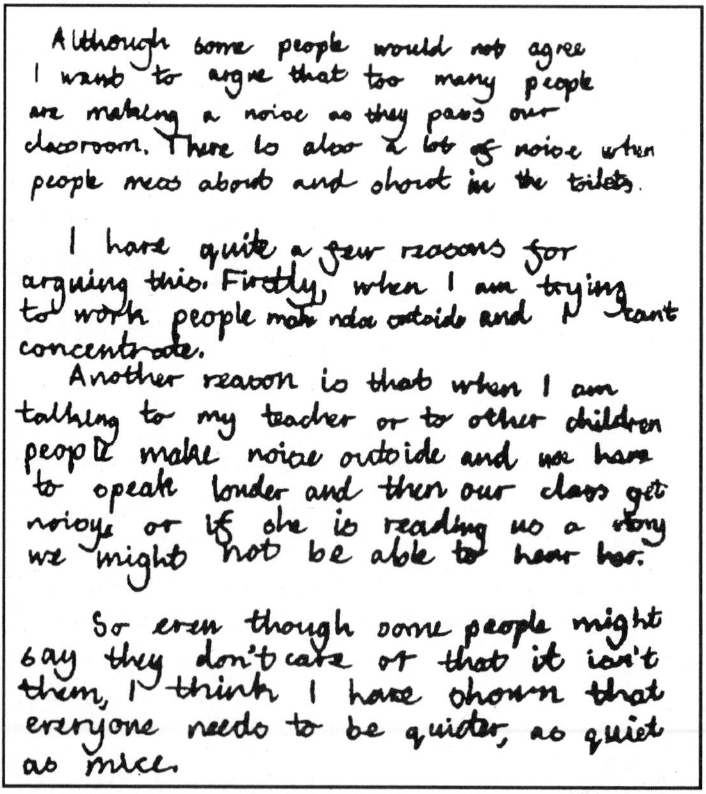
Although some people would not agree I want to argue that too many people are making a noise as they pass our classroom. There is also a lot of noise when people mess about and shout in the toilets.

I have quite a few reasons for arguing this. Firstly, when I am trying to work people make noise outside and I cant concentrate.

Another reason is that when I am talking to my teacher or to other children people make noise outside and we have to speak louder and then our class get noisy or if she is reading us a story we might not be able to hear her.

So even though some people might say they don't care or that it isn't them, I think I have shown that everyone needs to be quieter, as quiet as mice.

Figure 5.24. Writing to persuade the rest of the school to be quieter.

USING DISCUSSION FRAMES

Discussion is a genre that children are expected to use increasingly as they progress through the education system. Pupils in secondary and higher education have to write essays in which they weigh arguments backed by evidence before reaching a conclusion. And yet often have had very little experience of this form before they are required to use it themselves.

Oral debate is a feature of many primary classrooms, and with careful preparation, writing discussion papers can be a natural extension of this. After a discussion, or as an accompaniment to it, a preliminary framework like that shown in Figure 5.27 might be used. Teachers can make their own giant versions of this on sugar paper, or use a transparency for an overhead projector, in order to model the development of a series of discussion points. The frame can also be used as a focus for shared writing. Figures 5.25 and 5.26 show examples of frames used by children who had been on a visit to a local zoo. During the return journey a heated argument had broken out as to whether zoos were cruel or not and whether a safari park was 'better' than a zoo. When they got back to the classroom, the teacher seized the opportunity to develop the argument, first into a preliminary listing and then into the writing of discussion papers.

In their preliminary listing of ideas (Figure 5.25 shows an example), the children had difficulty in forming an initial statement that gave both sides of the argument. They decided to put 'Zoos are good'. When they came to develop pieces of writing, this initial statement of only one view caused them further problems. For example, one child first wrote 'There is a lot of argument about zoos being bad' – and then crossed out 'bad' and put 'good'. To overcome this kind of problem, we have since redesigned the discussion frames, rephrasing the opener as 'The issue we are discussing is whether...'. We have found that this almost obliges children to include both sides of a question in their opening statement.

The issue we are discussing is **Zoo's are Good**

Arguments for

① Zoo's are Good because the Animals can not be hunted ② Zoo's are Good because they feed the Animal's well ③ Zoo's are Good Because they can be Discoverd. I think that safari park's dearer than Zoo's

Arguments against

Safari Park's are Better than Zoos Because the Safari Park have more space For the Animals. ② Safari Park's are better Because they Don't keep the Animals in cages ③ Safari is Better Because In zoo's they can't be filmed

My conclusion

I think that zoo's are better places for animals than safari Park's. Because Animal can't be Hunted

Figure 5.25. A preliminary discussion frame.

There is a lot of argument about zoo's being ~~bad~~ good.

The people who agree with this idea, such as the zoo claim that Zoo's are good because the animals will not be hunted, and they get food regualy.

They also argue that Humans are safe from the animals that attac people.

A further point they make is the animals can not run away from ther cages and can not attack people. ~~The an~~ they can not get lost.

However there are also strong arguments against this point of view. I believe that zoo's are bad because it is not the animals normal habitat.

Another counter argument is that zoo's are bad and sifary parks are good.

Furthermore zoo's are bad because the animals have not got free space to run in but in sifary parks the animals have got a lot of space.

After looking at the different points of view and the evidence for them I think Zoo are bad because the animals have not got space to run and it in not the animals normal habitat

Figure 5.26. Discussion writing.

Children often find it difficult to see the 'other side' of an argument. Encouraging them to list ideas for and against a statement forces them to acknowledge that there is more than one point of view. Of course, this is more difficult where their emotions are involved. In the example given in Figure 5.27 the events under discussion were sufficiently remote for the child to be able to make a dispassionate listing of perceived advantages and disadvantages.

The issue we are discussing is

Whether the Roman invasion of Britain was a good thing.

Arguments for	Arguments against
They introduced better: roads Healthcare armour houshold things foods, Schooling. They built forts and houses They introduced reading & writing (didn't they?) They taught us to be better fighters. They brought us together. And after that they left everything for us.	They killed many of the British They took Britains and turned them into slaves. They took our crops & gold & silver They Destroyed the towns and villages.

My conclusion

Yes, because we have benifited from it.

Figure 5.27. Preliminary discussion frame.

We have shown a range of writing frames relating to the main non-fiction genres. In Chapter 6 we will look at how teachers can devise their own frames, and how they can use their knowledge of the language features of generic forms to discuss such features with their pupils as they write. We will consider the use of frames with children with special needs, and also suggest ways in which teachers might plan for a range of writing within their classrooms.

FURTHER ISSUES

USING WRITING FRAMES WITH CHILDREN WITH LEARNING DIFFICULTIES

The use of writing frames by children of widely differing abilities has been of great interest to us. Several teachers working with the EXEL project have special responsibility for supporting children with learning difficulties within mainstream schools. Most of these children have difficulties with reading and writing. Because our classrooms operate on the basis that children read and write across the curriculum, in maths, history, geography, science, and so on, these children with literacy problems face constant struggles. Most of them can only be given a few hours of individual support a week. Therefore, the special needs teachers working with our project wanted strategies to offer to their children which would also support them when adult attention wasn't available, and which the class teachers would be able to continue using within the normal classroom routines. Writing frames were found to give the children one such strategy, while also enabling them to achieve some success at writing: a vital ingredient in improving their self-esteem, and motivation.

Enumeration, sequential and *prior knowledge frames* (see Chapter 5) proved the most successful ones to introduce to these children since they direct attention clearly to the topic, and their personalised sentence structures make the writers active participants, using their own voices. One group of three special needs children watched a video with their class on 'Life in Tudor and Stuart Times'. Everyone was then asked to write about what they had seen. Normally, after a great deal of coaxing and encouragement, the three special needs children would have produced brief recounts. On this occasion, their support teacher used a *prior knowledge + reaction frame*. After discussion and teacher modelling of the frame, the children went on to write their own pieces. Figure 6.1 shows one boy's writing. It is extensive and coherent.

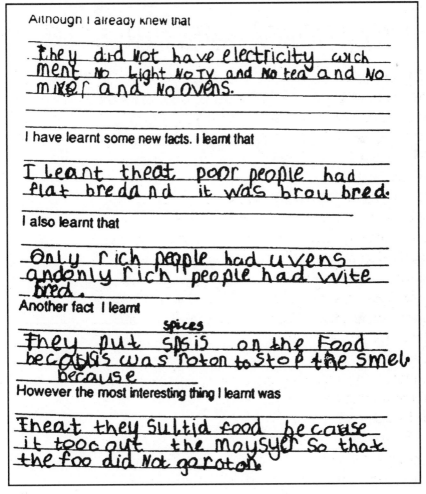

Although I already knew that

> They did not have electricity wich ment No Light No TV and No tea and No mixer and No ovens.

I have learnt some new facts. I learnt that

> I Leant theat poor people had flat bred and it was brou bred.

I also learnt that

> Only rich people had uvens andonly rich people had wite bred.

Another fact I learnt

> They put spsis on the Food becaus was roton to stop the smel because

However the most interesting thing I learnt was

> Theat they sultid food because it tooc out the mousyer So that the foo did Not go rotot.

Figure 6.1. Special needs child – Year 5.

By asking the children to think about what they already knew and what they learned, the frame encouraged them to re-order the information and demonstrate their understanding, rather than just recounting what they had seen.

Another advantage of writing frames for children with learning difficulties is that they avoid presenting the children

Before I began this topic I thought that I DID'T NO NOTN

But when I read about it I found out that teh rie ver Neire te h of M. Fladdid for three sip the ws.

I also learnt that teh mnmmy JK work

go

in bo r s s.

Furthermore I learnt that teh Gypsan Peopel uiste whsere marks.

Finally I learnt that

Figure 6.2. Framed writing by Scott – Year 3.
Before I began this topic I thought I didn't know nothing.
But when I read about it I found out that the river Nile flooded
for three weeks.
I also learned that the mummy go in boxes.
Furthermore I learned that the Egyptian people used to wear
masks.

with a blank sheet of paper – a particularly daunting experience for those accustomed to failure. With the support of a frame, many children achieved their most successful pieces of writing to date. One example is the work of a statemented child receiving extra help, shown in Figure 6.2. He and his support teacher were both thrilled by this, as it was the most extended piece of writing he had ever produced.

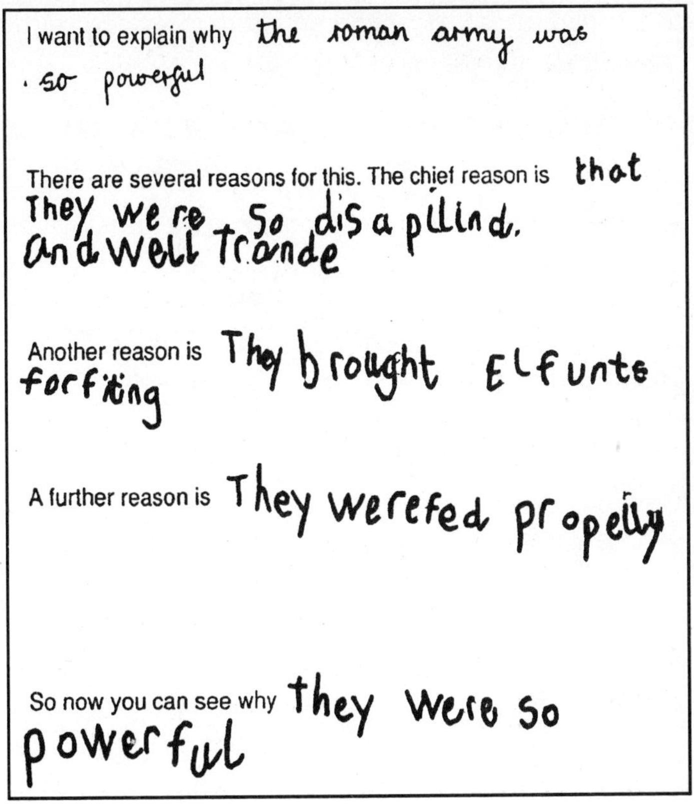

I want to explain why *the roman army was . so powerful*

There are several reasons for this. The chief reason is *that They we re so dis a pllind, and well trande*

Another reason is *for fixing They brought ELfunts*

A further reason is *They werefed propelly*

So now you can see why *they were so powerful*

Figure 6.3. Edward – Year 4. The first
sentence was scribed by the teacher.

The same kind of success has been reported to us by support teachers in mainstream schools, both primary and secondary, and in special schools.

Frames can also support children's attempts to write in an unfamiliar genre. Asking special needs children to write an explanation is to set them a difficult task. This type of writing needs to be structured in a logical way which will make sense. The inability to order their writing in sequential steps often leads children to produce incoherent explanations. The format of the frames demands that they think before they write and offers them support in organising their ideas.

We will be following these and other children's progress to see if their writing continues to improve. However, the value of supportive structures for children with learning difficulties certainly seems self-evident.

DISCUSSING LANGUAGE FEATURES

A writing frame is only intended to be used for a first draft of a piece of writing and we have already stressed that children should be encouraged to cross things out and add to and alter the frames to suit their individual needs. A completed framed draft can then serve as the basis for a conference on a child's writing, during which the language features of a genre can be discussed.

Sally and her class had been looking at the United Nations Declaration of Children's Rights, as part of their work on one of the cross-curricular themes of the National Curriculum. The class had discussed which other rights they felt should be added to the Declaration. One group of children used an argument frame to help structure their writing, and Sally's first draft is shown in Figure 6.4.

We can see that this is a deeply felt piece of writing. After discussing it and the emotions it contained with Sally, her teacher wanted both to develop Sally's writing of an argument and to help her use her personal experience to support a point of view. They talked about the idea of a 'declaration' being a document aimed at a wide audience of potential readers and therefore the appropriateness of making a general point first and then backing it up with personal evidence. They considered whether, to make a general point, you would use personal terms like 'I have' or universal terms like 'Children have'. Afterwards Sally redrafted her work (Figure 6.5).

Her completed writing shows how a powerful personal argument has been developed into a powerful general argument backed up by evidence. With just one minor slip, Sally has sustained the use of generic terms such as 'children' and 'they'.

Teachers can use the language features associated with each generic form to guide their conferences with writers. For example, they can discuss connectives with a child writing an

Although not every body would agree, I want to argue that I have rights not to have to drive 9 and a half hours to visit my gran in Norfolk. The drive is very boring and Ben, my brother, s always sick.

I have several reasons for arguing for this point of view. My first reason is that I have this thing about Ben being sick, for some strange reason it frightens me.

A further reason is that Gran just ignores me.

Furthermore I miss my mother terribly.

Therefore, although some people argue that I have to go,

I think I have shown that I have rights not to have to go.

Figure 6.4. Sally's first draft.

explanation, or talk about the difference between the imperative and the simple present as alternative ways of writing a procedure. Conferencing with children in this way means that language matters are taught at the 'point of usage' – that is, within the context of a real piece of writing being undertaken. Just as the frames themselves are not a reason for writing, so the analysis of language features given in Chapter 3 should not be used to give decontextualised skills lessons.

MOVING CHILDREN FROM THE FRAME TO INDEPENDENT WRITING

Once children are familiar with the form of a particular genre, they start to 'outgrow' the frame. This happens more quickly if they are encouraged to add to and alter the frame and generally

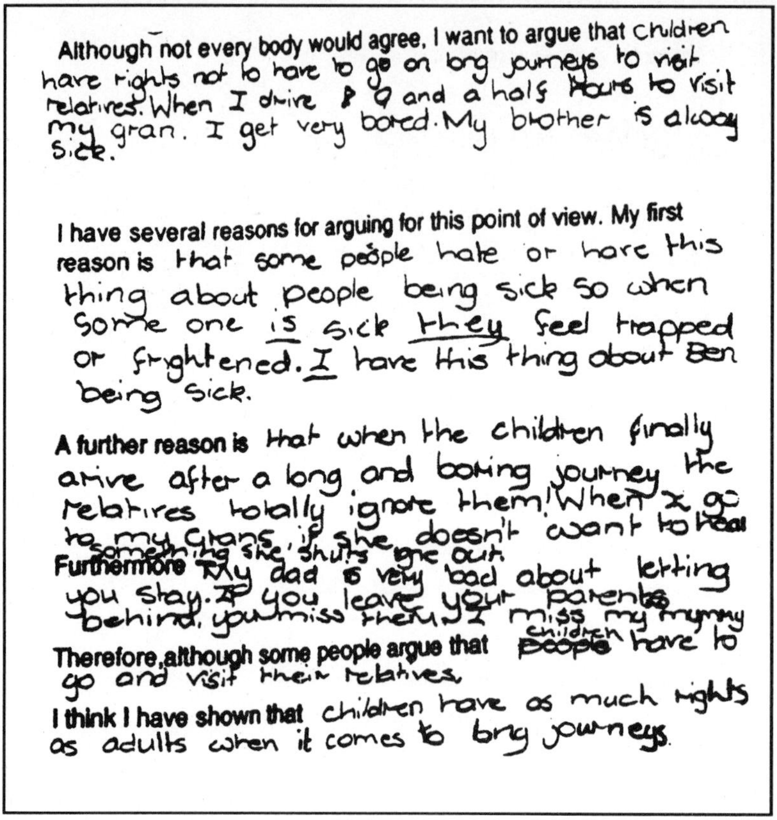

Although not every body would agree, I want to argue that children have rights not to have to go on long journeys to visit relatives. When I drive 8 9 and a half hours to visit my gran. I get very bored. My brother is alway sick.

I have several reasons for arguing for this point of view. My first reason is that some people hate or have this thing about people being sick so when some one is sick they feel trapped or frightened. I have this thing about Ben being sick.

A further reason is that when the children finally arive after a long and boring journey the relatives totally ignore them! When I go to my Grans, if she doesn't want to hear something she shuts me out.

Furthermore My dad is very bad about letting you stay. If you leave your parents behind, you miss them. I miss my mummy

Therefore, although some people argue that ~~people~~ children have to go and visit their relatives.

I think I have shown that children have as much rights as adults when it comes to long journeys.

Figure 6.5. Sally's second draft.

treat it as a drafting tool. Teachers should note whether the extended writing maintains its cohesive sense and pattern of connectives. For example, Robert, aged 9, had more to say about his trip to Dartmoor than the frame allowed and so he continued to add to it, as shown in Figure 6.6.

We can see that he continued to use appropriate connectives; his writing remained coherent. The structure of the frame had begun to give way to independent usage, suggesting that Robert was probably ready to move on to the independent phase. Of course, the length of time a pupil feels the need to use a frame will vary from individual to individual.

Children need to use the frames less and less, as their knowledge of the different genres increases. When children begin to show evidence of independent usage, the teacher may

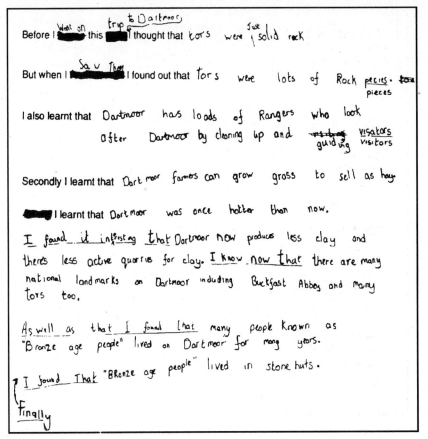

Before I ~~Went on~~ this ~~trip to Dartmoor~~ I thought that tors were ~~Just~~ solid rock

But when I ~~Saw That~~ I found out that Tors were lots of Rock pecies. ~~tors~~ / pieces

I also learnt that Dartmoor has loads of Rangers who look after Dartmoor by cleaning up and ~~visitors~~ visotors ~~guiding~~ visitors

Secondly I learnt that Dart moor farmers can grow gross to sell as hay.

~~■■■■~~ I learnt that Dartmoor was once hotter than now.

I found it intresting that Dartmoor now produces less clay and theres less active quarris for clay. I know now that there are many national landmarks on Dartmoor including Buckfast Abbey and many tors too.

As well as that I found that many people known as "Bronze age people" lived on Dartmoor for many years.

I found That "Bronze age people" lived in stone huts.

Finally

Figure 6.6. Robert's writing, with his independently added connectives underlined.

need only to have master copies of the frames available, as 'help cards' for when children need a prompt. A box of such help cards could be kept in the writing area, where children are encouraged to refer to many different writing aids. This fits with the general 'procedural facilitation' strategy for children's writing suggested by Bereiter and Scardamalia (1987). It also seems to be a way of encouraging children to begin to make independent decisions about their own learning.

When children do begin to write independently in particular genres it is often quite easy to see how they have assimilated both structure and vocabulary from the writing frames. The confidently written text shown in Figure 6.7 was composed

Our class have been debating whether football should only be allowed to be played in the school playground on Mondays, Wednesdays and Fridays because our playground is quite small in the winter when we can't use the field.

The people who don't like playing football say it is unfair that football takes up a lot of space in the playground. They say they cannot walk around because they get bumped into and hit with the ball. They also say it is scarey for little kids.

The footballers say that most people like playing so they should be allowed to. And if they cannot practise the school team will get worse and we won't win many games. Also they will not enjoy school if they cannot play with their friends.

I think that football should be allowed every day because most people like it and it is good fun.

Figure 6.7. Independent discussion writing after previous experience of framed discussion writing. Year 6. This script was typed up on the computer by the child after the child had written a first draft.

without the direct guidance of a frame. The writer had previously been working on the discussion genre, through shared and framed writing.

PLANNING FOR WRITING IN A RANGE OF GENRES

We have said many times that writing in a particular genre should occur when a reason arises to use that genre. But that does not mean that teaching writing has to be entirely random and opportunistic! Opportunities to develop writing in a particular genre do arise spontaneously, and teachers have always exploited such occasions. For example, in Chapter 6, we saw how a teacher recognised and seized the chance to use the discussion genre after a visit to the zoo. However, it is also quite possible to plan opportunities for children to write in a

Local Area Study

Recount
- history of the school, local church, etc.
- life story of any famous local people
- memories of elder residents

Procedure
- how to get from home to school
- how to apply for membership of the local sports club
- recipes for local dishes

Persuasive argument
- argue for a better park
- argue for the pedestrianising of local roads

Report
- survey of local shops
- comparison of buildings
- report on local families

Explanation
- why did the town grow where it did?
- why are most of the local houses built of granite?

Discussion
- discuss the arguments for and against the siting of a new supermarket
- discuss whether local rubbish should be recycled, in spite of the expense

Figure 6.8. Planning for writing in a range of genres.

range of genres. Indeed, if the balance of children's writing is to be corrected by reducing the overwhelming preponderance of recount writing, it is probably essential that this be done.

We asked several groups of teachers to brainstorm around the National Curriculum history and geography topics that they were planning to use in the near future, in order to see what non-fiction writing genres they could plan as a natural part of this work. Two examples of such planning are given in Figures 6.8 and 6.9.

Another approach would be to decide to concentrate on a particular genre over the course of a few weeks and to plan

The Tudors

Persuasive argument
- Elizabeth I was a great monarch
- England became a settled country for the first time under the Tudors

Procedure
recipes for
- food
- herbal medicines
- make-up
- how to make a pomander

Recount
- visits to museums, etc
- Drake's diary
- Tudor Christmas

Report
comparative reports
- Tudor food/our food
- houses
- clothes

Explanation
- explain why Henry founded the Church of England
- explain why Mary Queen of Scots was kept prisoner

Discussion
- discuss whether Henry VIII was right to dissolve the monasteries
- discuss whether he was a good husband
- discuss whether the Poor Laws were fair and reasonable

Figure 6.9. Planning for writing in a range of genres.

opportunities to use that genre in all areas of the curriculum. For example, if it was decided to focus on explanations, the following tasks might be included:

Maths – explain what makes a square or a triangle;

Science – explain why we have night and day;

Geography – explain why the local town is situated where it is;

History – explain why the Vikings invaded Britain;

R.E. – explain the significance of certain holy artefacts;

Art – explain why Impressionist paintings were considered
so shocking;

Technology – explain why one design is better than
another.

Both these planning approaches have value and they should
be used to make sure that children get full experience of writing
in a range of non-fiction genres. This is much too important to
be left only to chance!

WRITING YOUR OWN FRAMES

Once familiar with the structures and language features of
various genres, you can begin to devise your own frames
specific to your own pupils. You can also move away from the
broad categories discussed in this book, to frame other non-
fiction categories.

Producing frames requires a wide knowledge of connectives –
of the ways in which ideas are linked in writing to create a
coherent whole. The following are some of the main linking
words and phrases. For a more comprehensive list see Parker
(1993), on whose analysis parts of the list below are based.

CAUSAL CONNECTIVES

because, therefore, thus, so, as a result, as a result of which,
consequently, thanks to, for, then, in view of which, which
makes.

TEMPORAL CONNECTIVES

1. Following on: then, next, by and by, in due course,
eventually, finally, at length, in the end, thereafter, later, after
that, subsequently
2. Prior: before, at first, to begin with, in the beginning, until
(then), by (then), up to that time, hitherto,
3. At the same time: meanwhile, simultaneously, all the while,
in the meantime, concurrently.

CONTRADICTIVE CONNECTIVES

but, on the other hand, a counter argument, against that, instead

CONTRASTIVE CONNECTIVES

however, yet, nevertheless, notwithstanding, for all that, in contrast, looking at it another way

REFERRING BACK CONNECTIVES (ANAPHORA)

the above, those, the forgoing, this, that, these, such

REFERRING FORWARDS CONNECTIVES (CATAPHORA)

the following, as follows, below, this, these, here, thus, like this, in this way

There are other categories of connectives including disjunctive (indeed) and reformulation (in other words), amongst others (Parker, 1993) and you will probably be able to add your own further words and phrases to the categories listed more above. Those listed however should provide the skeleton for your own frames because of the vital role they play in maintaining cohesion.

POINTS TO REMEMBER

We hope that you will find writing frames useful in helping children towards independent non-fiction writing. Remember:

✦ Use of a frame should always begin with discussion and teacher modelling. Then move on to joint construction (teacher + child/group) before the children undertake their own writing supported by the frame.

✦ Not all the children in a class will need to use a writing frame.

✦ A frame should be introduced to give extra support when a need arises to write in a particular genre. The frame in itself is never a reason for writing.

✦ It should be made clear to the children that the frame is just a draft. They should be encouraged to cross out, amend and add to the frame, as suits them.

✦ Frames are only a small part of the rich and varied writing experience we should offer children. They need wide experience of text written in a range of genres, as well as opportunities to write in a variety of contexts.

✦ Generic structures are not rigid, unchangeable forms. It is not appropriate to teach them in this way.

✦ The frames in this book are starting points. Teachers can use their knowledge of generic structures to devise frames for their own unique classroom contexts and purposes.

BIBLIOGRAPHY

Anderson, R.C. (1977) 'The Notion of Schemata and the Educational Enterprise' from Anderson, R.C., Spiro, R.J. and Montaque, W.E. (Eds.) *Schooling and the Acquisition of Knowledge*, Hillsdale, N J: Lawrence Erlbaum.

 Anderson, T.H. and Armbruster, B.B. (1981) *Content Area Textbooks Reading Report No 24*, University of Illinois: Center for the Study of Reading.

Anderson, R.C. and Pearson, P.D. (1984) 'A Schema-Theoretical View of Basic Processes in Reading Comprehension' from Pearson, P.D. (Ed.) *Handbook of Reading Research*, New York: Longman.

Barrs, M. (1991/92) 'Genre Theory. What's it all about?', *Language Matters*, No 1. 5–16, London: CLPE.

Beard, R. (1984) *Children's Writing in the Primary School*, London: UKRA/ Hodder and Stoughton.

Bereiter, C. and Scardamalia, M. (1985) 'Children's Difficulties in Learning to Compose' from Wells, G. and Nicholls, J. (Eds.) *Language and Learning: An Interactive Perspective*, Basingstoke: Falmer Press.

Bereiter, C. and Scardamalia, M. (1987) *The Psychology of Written Composition*, Hillsdale, N J: Lawrence Erlbaum.

Bereiter, C. and Scardamalia, M. (1982) 'From Conversation to Composition: The Role of Instruction in a Developmental Process' from Glaser, R. (Ed.) *Advances in Instructional Psychology, Vol 2*, London: Lawrence Erlbaum Associates.

Bransford, J. (1983) 'Schema Activation – Schema Acquisition' from Anderson, R.C., Osborn, J. and Tierney, R.J. (Eds.) *Learning to Read in American Schools*, Hillsdale, NJ: Lawrence Erlbaum.

Britton, J. (1972) *Language and Learning*, Harmondsworth: Penguin Books.

Britton, J. et al. (1975) *The Development of Writing Abilities 11–18*, Basingstoke: Macmillan.

Cairney, T. (1990) *Teaching Reading Comprehension*, Milton Keynes: Open University Press.

Cairney, T. (1992) 'Mountain or Mole Hill: The Genre Debate Viewed from Down Under', *Reading*, 26.(1), 23–29.

Calkins, L. (1983) *Lessons from a Child*, Portsmouth, N H : Heinemann.

Callaghan, M. and Rothery, J. (1988) *Teaching Factual Writing: A Genre Based Approach. Report of the DSP Literacy Project*, Sydney: Metropolitan East Region, NSW Department of Education.

Chapman, J. (1983) *Reading Development and Cohesion*, London: Heinemann.

Christie, F. (1984) (Ed.) *Children Writing: Study Guide*, Geelong: Deakin University Press.

Clegg, A. (Ed.) (1965) *The Excitement of Writing*, London: Chatto and Windus.

Collerson, J. (1988) (Ed.) *Writing for Life*, Sydney: PETA.

Cudd, E.T. and Roberts, L. (1989) 'Using Writing to Enhance Content Area Learning in the Primary Grades,' *The Reading Teacher*, Vol 42. No 6, 392–404.

DES (1975) *A Language for Life*, (The Bullock Report), London: HMSO.

DES (1989) *English in the National Curriculum (No 1)*, London: HMSO.

DES (1990) *English in the National Curriculum (No 2)*, London: HMSO.

DES (1992) *The Implementation of the Curricular Requirements of the Education Reform Act: English Key Stages 1, 2 and 3. A report by H M Inspectorate on the second year 1990–91*, London: HMSO.

DFE (1995) *English in the National Curriculum*, London: HMSO.

Department of Employment, Education and Training (1989) *A Brief Introduction to Genre*, Sydney: Language and Social Power Project, Metropolitan East Disadvantaged Schools Program.

Derewianka, B. (undated) *The LINC Model of Language: a discussion paper*, Slough: Centre for Research in Language and Communication, NFER.

Derewianka, B. (1990) *Exploring How Texts Work*, Newtown, NSW: PETA.

Graves, D. (1983) *Writing: Teachers and Children at Work*, Portsmouth, N H: Heinemann.

Hall, N. (1987) *The Emergence of Literacy*, Sevenoaks: Hodder and Stoughton.

Halliday, M.A.K. (1975) *Learning How to Mean: Explorations in the Development of Language*, London: Arnold.

Halliday, M.A.K. (1978) *Language as a Social Semiotic: The Theoretical Interpretation of Language and Meaning*, London: Arnold.

Halliday, M.A.K. (1985) *An Introduction to Functional Grammar*, London: Arnold.

Halliday, M.A.K. and Hasan, R. (1976) *Cohesion in English*, London: Longman.

Harrison, A. and McEvedy, M. R. (1987) *From Speech to Writing*, Malvern, Australia: Robert Anderson and Associates.

Harste, J., Woodward, V. and Burke, C. (1984) *Language Stories and Literacy Lessons*, Portsmouth, N H: Heinemann.

Kress, G. (1982) *Learning to Write*, London: Routledge.

Kress, G. (1987) 'Genre in a Social Theory of Language' from Reid (Ed.) *The Place of Genre in Learning*, Sydney: Deakin University Press.

Kress, G. and Knapp, P. (1992) 'Genre in a Social Theory of Language', *English in Education*, 26. (2), 5–15.

Lane, S.M. and Kemp, M. (1967) *An Approach to Creative Writing in the Primary School*, London: Blackie.

Lave, J. and Wenger, E. (1991) *Situated Learning*, Cambridge: Cambridge University Press.

Lewis, M., Wray, D. and Rospigliosi, P. (1995) '"No copying please!" Helping children respond to non-fiction text' *Education 3–13*, 23 (1), 27–34.

Lewis, M. and Wray, D. (1995) *Teachers' Views on Reading and Writing. EXEL Working Paper No 9*, Exeter: EXEL Project, University of Exeter.

Littlefair, A.B. (1991) *Reading All Types of Writing*, Milton Keynes: Open University Press.

Littlefair, A.B. (1992) *Genres in the Classroom*, Minibook 1, Warrington: UKRA.

Lunzer, E. and Gardner, K. (1984) *Learning from the Written Word*, Edinburgh: Oliver and Boyd.

Macken, M. et al (1989) *The theory and practice of genre based writing*, Sydney: Literacy and Education Research Network, Directorate of Studies, NSW Department of Education.

Martin, J.R., Christie, F. and Rothery, J. (1987) 'Social Processes in Education' from Reid (Ed.) *The Place of Genre in Learning*, Sydney: Deakin University Press.

Martin, J.R. and Rothery, J. (1980, 1981, 1986) *Writing Project Report, Nos. 1, 2 and 4*, Sydney: Department of Linguistics, University of Sydney.

Maybury, B. (1967) *Creative Writing for Juniors*, London: Batsford.

Meek, M. (1988) *How Texts Teach What Readers Learn*, Stroud: Thimble Press.

Newman, J. (1984) *The Craft of Children's Writing*, Richmond Hill, Ontario: Scholastic–TAB.

OFSTED (1993) *The Implementation of the Curricular Requirements of the Education Reform Act: English Key Stages 1, 2, 3 and 4. Fourth year, 1992–93. A Report from the Office of Her Majesty's Chief Inspector of Schools*, London: HMSO.

Parker, S. (1993) *The Craft of Writing*, London: Paul Chapman.

Perera, K. (1984) *Children's Reading and Writing*, Oxford: Blackwell.

Rothery, J. (1984) 'The Development of Genres – Primary to Junior Secondary School' from *Language Studies: Children's Writing: Study Guide*, Sydney: Deakin University Press.

Rothery, J. (1985) *Teaching Writing in the Primary School: A Genre-Based Approach to the Development of Writing Abilities*, Sydney: Department of Linguistics, University of Sydney.

Stratta, L. and Dixon, J. (1992) 'The National Curriculum in English: Does Genre Theory Have Anything to Offer?', *English in Education*, 26. (2), 16–27.

Stewart, O. and Tei, E. (1984) 'Some Implications of Metacognition for Reading Instruction', *Journal of Reading*, 27, 36–43.

Stewart-Dore, N. (Ed.) (1986) *Writing and Reading to Learn*, Sydney: PETA.

Teale, W. and Sulzby, E. (1986) *Emergent Literacy: Writing and Reading*, Norwood, NJ: Ablex.

Vygotsky, L. (1978) *Mind in Society: The Development of Higher Psychological Processes*, Cambridge, Mass: Harvard University Press.

Wells, G. (1987) *The Meaning Makers*, London: Hodder and Stoughton.

Wilson, P.T. and Anderson, R.C. (1986) 'What they don't know will hurt them: the role of Prior Knowledge in Comprehension' from Orasanu, J. (Ed.) *Reading Comprehension: from Research into Practice*, Hillsdale, NJ: Lawrence Erlbaum.

Wing Jan, L. (1991) *Write Ways. Modelling Writing Forms*, Melbourne: Oxford University Press.

Winograd, P. and Bridge, C. (1986) 'The comprehension of important information in written prose' from Baumann, J.F. and Newark, D.E. (Ed.) *Teaching Main Idea Comprehension*, International Reading Association.

Wray, D. and Medwell, J. (1991) *Literacy and Language in the Primary Years*, London: Routledge.

INDEX

Note: References in italic indicate pages containing illustrated examples.